THE GREED SYNDROME

THE GREED SYNDROME

AN ETHICAL SICKNESS
IN AMERICAN CAPITALISM

by J. Arthur Baird

Hampshire Books
Akron ● Philadelphia
1989

Scripture quotations from the Revised Standard Version of the Bible are copyright, 1946, 1952, and 1971, by the Division of Christian Education of the National Council of Churches of Christ in the U. S. A., and are used by permission.

Cover design: Richard Kish

Library of Congress Cataloging-in-Publication Data

Baird, J. Arthur (Joseph Arthur)
   The greed syndrome: an ethical sickness in American capitalism / by J. Arthur Baird.
       p.   cm.
   ISBN 1-877674-02-8
   1. Capitalism — United States — Moral and ethical aspects.
2. Capitalism — United States — Religious aspects.   I. Title
HB501.B225 1989
174'.4 — dc20   89-15284
                                                                        CIP

Printed in the United States of America.

*Dedicated to the
Wooster Lay Academy of Religion*

CONTENTS

A syndrome is a pattern of symptoms typical of a particular disease. (Webster)

Greed is a moral disease whose symptoms are all around us, combining into a social syndrome that is threatening the health of our nation.

Be warned, O Jerusalem,
lest I be alienated from you...
"For from the least to the greatest of them,
every one is greedy for unjust gain;
and from prophet to priest,
every one deals falsely...
Therefore they shall fall among those who fall;
at the time that I punish them,
they shall be overthrown," says the Lord. (Jeremiah 6:8-15)

He has showed you, O man, what is good;
and what does the Lord require of you
but to do justice, and to love kindness,
and to walk humbly with your God? (Micah 6:8)

Therefore do not be anxious,
saying, 'What shall we eat?'
or 'What shall we wear?'...
your heavenly Father knows
that you need them all.
But seek first his kingdom
and his righteousness,
and all these things shall be yours as well. (Matt. 6:31-33)

Preface

This is a book about an ethical crisis which seems to be occurring in America in the latter days of the twentieth century. Our point of focus will be on the economic sector, with special attention to the phenomenon of greed; but the larger concern is for the moral disease which has spread into all aspects of our society, of which greed is only one part. Morality has come into special prominence in recent months, and will therefore serve especially well to highlight the more pervasive problem.

The ethical issues of greed are too vast for this to be an exhaustive treatment. It is rather a selective focusing on certain representative problems in order to reveal the trend and discover a viable ethic for American democratic capitalism. So I concentrate on ethics and economics from a theological perspective. All the case studies included here which describe the operation of greed are aimed primarily at this ethical focus.

As we analyze the Greed phenomena, we will be aiming primarily at therapy because that is what is most desperately needed. We can analyze the illness to death while the patient slowly succumbs before us. It is an attempt to describe an ethic that works because it is in tune with the imperatives of God's justice which transcend personal opinion and the changing social climate. Robert Bellah's instincts are on target: we do need to rediscover the Biblical tradition in order to ground our values in spiritual insights that transcend the interests of individuals. (*Habits of the Heart*) It is curious that it is professional sociologists, Jew, Christian, secular, who are recalling us to the need for transcendent ethical values.

Most especially, I am going to suggest that the Christian version of this ethic is especially suited to this ostensibly Christian, but highly varied nation. Jesus was a Jew, speaking to men and women in one of the most sophisticated, secular, pluralistic, religiously complex cultures in history. He spoke of that mixed heritage with sympathy as well as criticism. His message of the kingdom of God has a way of transcending any age or religious organization that tries to acculturate or captivate his theology and ethic.

In my presentation of the Biblical God, I will follow the practice of Jesus in referring to God as father in the male gender. This is a complicated question, and one that has properly been raised within the current feminist movement. What I have done here is to be scrupulous in including both men and women in my language about the human scene, and to that end have slightly re-translated some Biblical passages.

When I refer to morality and ethics, I will be using the terms interchangeably. Ethics comes from the Greek *ethos*, and refers to how we act in our social setting. The word morality comes from the Latin *mores*, and again means simply how we act in our cultural context. At the level of language, they are neutral terms and can refer to any kind of ethic from Christian to barbarian. What we have to do is fill them with content and decide what type of behavior we are talking about. At that point we are in the discipline of ethics and inevitably dealing with certain religious ideas that stand behind it.

I am defining a syndrome as a pattern of symptoms typical of a particular disease. I identify greed as a moral or ethical disease whose symptoms are all around us, combining into a social syndrome that threatens the health of our nation.

This has been a collective project. I feel as if a small army of people has been gathering data on this subject and feeding it to me. Beyond the excellent work of the investigative journalism of the news media and professional papers, magazines and books, there are many individuals, too numerous to mention, who have, out of their own experiences, given me illustrations of the phenomena herein described. They write me, phone me or stop me in the street with yet another tale more bizarre than the last. There are some who must be mentioned, and these are the participants in the Lay Academy of Religion at the College of Wooster in the fall of 1986 whose lectures on the subject of "The Greed Syndrome" have informed this book on every page. Where I have borrowed directly, their contributions are acknowledged. Mostly they have provided a general deepening of my own thought which is too subtle and pervasive to document specifically.

Special thanks then go to Prof. David Guldin, Dept. of Sociology, the College of Wooster, Stephen De John, Ohio State Lottery Commission, The Rev. Michael Lavell, S.J., Vice President for Academic Affairs, John Carroll University, Cleveland, Professor William Baird, Dept. of Economics, The College of Wooster, Professor Eugene Beem, lecturer on business ethics, Baldwin Wallace College, Ohio, the Hon. John R. Milligan, The Ohio Court of Appeals, Fifth District, Mr. Harry Featherstone, President, The Will Burt Co., Orrville, Ohio, Professor Laurence Vande Creek, lecturer on Medical Ethics, OSU School of Medicine, Columbus, Mr. Charles W. Landefeld esq., Arter & Hadden Attorneys at Law, Cleveland, Professor Lucy Bregman, Dept. of Religion, Temple University, Philadelphia, Mr. Philip Howes esq., Vogelsang, Howes, Lindamood & Brunn, Attorneys at Law, Canton, Ohio.

I would add four others who have been most helpful, but were not part of the Lay Academy: Donald Noble, board chairman and C.E.O. (retired) of Rubbermaid Corporation, Stanley Gault, C.E.O. Rubbermaid and president (1987) of the National Association of Manufacturers, Timothy Smucker, chairman, J.M. Smucker Co., and Professor Edward Long, Madison, N.J. It is with such persons, along with the large and dedicated group of lay men and women who attended this series, that the hope for the ethical future of America will lie. I am encouraged, but there is much work to be done.

J. Arthur Baird
Wooster, Ohio

Chapter 1

Introduction
A Generation on the Take

With all its affluence, America ought to be the happiest nation on earth. And in many ways we are, with a vitality that still testifies to our national youth. But something is wrong. We are living in a strange age where undreamed of things are happening. We are in the midst of a series of bizarre symptoms that have caught the attention of the nation. Some of these symptoms are ugly, like the eruption of a gruesome cancer, and there is no question they must be cut out.

There are many manifestations of this illness, but some of the most dramatically visible are in the area of economics. Every one of the media is flooding us with a whole new vocabulary to describe this situation: corporate raiders, greenmail, arbitrageurs, insider trading, stock churning, leverage buy-outs, deep pockets, contingency fees, malpractice, junk bonds, tort liability. The list is endless, and we wonder what is going on and how serious it is.

Greed Rules

One word continues to surface as a general label for what

many consider to be the controlling infection: GREED. Russell
Baker, columnist for the New York Times Service, recently did
an article entitled "Greed Rules, at Least Nowadays." The
point was that "nowadays it is all right to want it all." This is
because, in the words of a current beer commercial, "You can
have it all." This is a highly researched description of one
aspect of the current American mentality, and they are probably right. As the managing editor of *Money* magazine recently
put it, "Money has come to be the number one obsession of
Americans."

TV is a fairly good mirror of American life and it is filled
with examples of this fixation. The "Wheel of Fortune" and the
"Lifestyles of the Rich and the Famous" dominate the air-
waves as they do our political and social lives generally. A
reporter for *Newsweek* magazine, on "This Week with David
Brinkley," recently expressed a common view that "the whole
tax reform movement was sparked by the acceleration of tax
cheating which is destroying our tax system, based as it has
been on the traditional honesty of Americans."

On a superficial level, these symptoms would appear to be
extreme examples of tactical problems that can be solved by
appropriate legislation. Robert Lekachman for example, in his
book *Greed Is Not Enough*, blames the problems of the U.S.
economy on supply-side "Reaganomics," looking nostalgically
at the demand-side economics of Franklin Roosevelt, the New
Deal and John Maynard Keynes, properly domesticated. Economic tactics are certainly an important part of the picture. But
I am suggesting here that our economic problems are much
more complicated than this, involving not only economic tactics, but also social, ethical and religious strategies and
ideologies that are much more subtle, powerful, long range
and personal. At a deeper level, what we will be examining in
these pages are symptoms of a widespread ethical sickness
which has been progressing for a long time and is just now
coming to particular focus in the social and especially economic life of our nation. As the most affluent nation on earth,
we are overfed; yet, curiously, we are showing what I would call

symptoms of undernourishment, of social, ethical, religious, as well as economic starvation.

Robert Bellah calls this "the poverty of affluence," in *Habits of the Heart*, one of the most widely read recent attempts to analyze our social situation. Bellah points to "self actualization" as the typical goal of middle class Americans and characterizes our culture as "utilitarian expressive individualism." He means that we are all out to get as much as possible for ourselves. The dead end of this radical individualism is the prevailing ethical relativism, "the loss of any objectifiable criteria for choosing one value over another." What this spells is moral chaos, the loss of meaning and coherence in society. Bellah quotes Madison, Toqueville and others to the effect that "the survival of a free people depends on the revival of public virtue that is able to find public expression." For Bellah, this calls for a "revival of the Biblical tradition to ground our values in spiritual insights that transcend the interests of individuals," a surprising statement from a team of university sociologists.

Daniel Bell, Harvard sociologist, widely hailed as one of the most important social thinkers of our time, in his book *The Cultural Contradictions of Capitalism*, comes to the same conclusion that hedonism, the pursuit of pleasure and avoidance of pain, is the prevailing value of our society. In the early development of capitalism, the unrestrained economic impulse was held in check by Puritan restraint and what is often called the Protestant Ethic. But this ethic has been undermined by capitalism itself, producing many contradictions within our society. Mass production and mass consumption have produced a hedonism which has rejected what he calls "the transcendental ethic" and any standards of ultimate meaning and substituted for it "the megalomania of self infinitization." This is just a complicated way of describing the infinite extension of our pride and self-interest, that is, of our greed. Again, we find a major sociologist describing the ethical relativism of much of current America where the only acceptable standard of value is one's own opinion. This he calls

"modernism." He finds its most recent epitome in the psyche-
delic pursuit of pleasure of the 1960s. Within the economic
sector, this has produced a strange contradiction. The new
capitalism continues to demand the exercise of the Protestant
Ethic in the area of production, but has stimulated the demand
for pleasure in the area of consumption, producing some bizarre symptoms. This, according to Bell, has been coming for
many years; but these radically visible contradictions from the
lack of any coherent moral or philosophical doctrine have only
become manifest today.

This is what Robert Benne, a social theologian, in *The
Ethic of Democratic Capitalism*, calls "Marketing Hedonism,"
and Eugene Borowitz, Professor of Education and Jewish
Thought at Hebrew Union College in New York, describes as
the "moral stagnation" in our beloved country. America has
"lost its heart" morally and religiously and transferred its trust
in God to a "trust in ever greater affluence." Howard Garner,
Professor of Education at the Virginia Commonwealth University, calls us "the rip-off generation" and describes the displacement of our traditional ethics by a new collective
behavior, that of "the society on the take," where the end
justifies the means and the pursuit of quick wealth is the norm.
He points to three high-status vocations, medicine, law and
politics, which have now been publicly labeled, whether fairly
or not, as being "on the take." Rightly or wrongly, the ambulance chasers are becoming the symbol for the modern legal
profession. One must assume that something is wrong.

All of this I am calling The Greed Syndrome. Those doing
social analyses of the situation are generally good at pathology.
And there is a surprising agreement among them over the
nature of the disease. But they also tend to agree in falling
short in the area of therapy. We are better quarterbacks on
Monday morning than Saturday afternoon. The problem is that
for us the game is still going on. When Bellah or Bell or
Borowitz or Benne or others point to our moral confusion, the
question is, what exactly do they mean? What moral standards
are being abandoned? What is their justification in the first

place? To what are we recalling this crazily plunging society which seems on a dizzying raft trip down some economic Grand Canyon with the threat of an awesome waterfall thundering in the distance?

Some Ethical Tools

In analyzing a complex issue like the Greed Syndrome, one of the problems lies in sorting out what one is doing. It is not clear just what we mean when we say that something is an ethical problem. The difficulty is that ethical questions having to do with how we ought to act within our ethos operate on at least three different levels: ideology, strategy and tactics. All three are involved in examining any one issue. We need to know where we are within the process.

Ideologies involve our most deeply held basic assumptions and lie behind all that we think and do. They almost inevitably raise the question of whether or not there is some absolute ethical standard, which is ultimately a theological question involving the existence and nature of God. It is usually only philosophers and theologians who raise these questions. But of all the questions one could ask, these are the most decisive for achieving justice, prosperity and happiness. Aristotle used to say that an unexamined life isn't worth living. What I am saying is that an unexamined ethic isn't worth having.

Strategies deal with what we mean by saying something "works." A strategy therefore has to do with the principles which emerge from one's basic ideology. These are what the ethicist calls "middle axioms" and are helpful in making a large ideology available for practical application. This is a very important level of the discussion, but one that is seldom considered.

Tactical questions have to do with the details of how a particular set of strategies work and usually don't go much beyond the practical level. These are the nuts and bolts of the question, and it is here that most so-called ethical discussion takes place.

Summarizing the Argument

In describing the Greed Syndrome as it operates within a series of case studies, I shall be showing that greed is quite a different thing from a valid self-interest and a responsible concern for profit. It is only when these become ethically pathological, when they feed upon themselves and produce symptoms of social illness, that we are talking about the "Greed Syndrome."

This ethical malaise operates subtly and pervasively within our American culture. It is especially contagious at the points of our contact with power, popularity and wealth. It operates within business and politics, within labor and management, throughout all the professions, whether secular or religious.

Two attitudes are absolutely basic to the Greed Syndrome: the primacy of material values, and the autonomy of human economic activity. In this kind of social climate, it is the higher values like idealism, unselfishness, justice, love that become either completely eclipsed, or subservient to those of a raging egocentric individualism whose blind struggle for survival and supremacy resembles the law of the jungle. Our question as humans with ethically responsible natures is how does our ethic handle an economy based so thoroughly on self-interest? One of our greatest needs is to bring the ethical state of our nation into conscious discussion. So this book is an exercise in ethical consciousness-raising which attempts to go beyond the pathological job of identifying and diagnosing the symptoms to the therapeutic task of proposing ethical treatment.

Any ethical analysis of the American economy must begin with the realization that capitalism is a relatively modern invention. It stems primarily from the thought of the Protestant reformer, John Calvin, with his belief in the dignity of the common man or woman, the ethical viability of self-interest, and the religious acceptability of economic activity, all under the sovereignty of God. It was Calvin's commitment to the absolute supremacy of God that provided the restraints on self-interest vitally necessary to making capitalism work.

What has happened, however, is that over the years America has lost this religious, God-centered commitment. Our motto of a nation "under God" has become a vestigial remnant of a once vital force which remains as an ideal or a fading echo within a thoroughly secular economy. The historical cause of the Greed Syndrome is the loss of Calvin's sovereign God, whose justice puts restraints on the overweening greed of the human animal. The Greed Syndrome, then, is ultimately a symptom of a largely unconscious but deeply imbedded atheism operating at all levels of society, but with special force in the area of economics.

The combination of the loss of God in modern society, the shift towards self-fulfillment in the work ethic and the return of laissez-faire economics is clearly the climate that has fueled the upsurge of greed in this decade. The thesis of these pages is that there is only one force in the universe capable of controlling, directing and chastening the inordinate and insatiable self-interest of the human animal. That is the sovereign God. Therein lies our hope.

When it comes to applying such an ethic to the many problem areas of our economy, the ideology of a nation "under God" needs to be brought into clear focus and then sharpened into ethical strategies and tactics in order for it to work in treating the pathological symptoms I shall be describing. Throughout this study, two controlling Biblical motifs will be operating. These are the sovereignty of God and the justice of God. It is they which form the ideological basis of the Biblical ethic, and dominate the strategies and tactics that are its blood, bone and sinew.

Beginning at a common level, we will be examining the Greed Syndrome in the areas of the consumer mentality and the salary structure in which we are all involved. We seem to be a nation dedicated to making as much money as we can as quickly as possible. This is manifest in a multitude of ways, from the evangelical zeal of the "Amway Community" to the promoters of the lottery fever. Salaries are a particularly sensitive barometer and the upward pressure for more is intense. Many ethical questions arise: what does this say about the disparity between poverty and wealth in our economy, about our system of values and about the status of the Protestant work ethic in America? How does the Hebrew-Christian ethic respond to the exploitation of chance, in the lottery, or on Wall Street?

Corporate America is facing threats from many directions. An ethical analysis suggests that in its desperation to meet these challenges, the business world is in danger of falling prey to the Greed Syndrome which is a formula for disaster. There is a new breed of merger manipulators who are threatening to undo the very corporate success they are trying so desperately to preserve. The Biblical ethic suggests that if and when these various approaches violate the justice of God, if short term solutions take precedence over long range ones, if profit becomes more important than persons, if narrowly defined individual concerns take precedence over the general welfare, then in the long run these will not work. What works from this ethical standpoint is that which is in tune with the sovereignty and justice of God.

The shift of the economic center from basic industry to investment banking has opened up fabulous new possibilities for good or evil. This new situation has spawned an entire generation of ethical questions dealing with the separation of legality from justice, the balancing of freedom and restraint, and the relation of short to long term policies. There is a war going on in the economic scene driven by corporate raiders and their allies, investment bankers. The outcome is the dismemberment of some of America's largest companies, an unhealthy increase in the amount of debt they carry, and damage to shareholders, employees and local communities. The October 1987 market crash dramatically demonstrated that the economy is much more fragile and vulnerable than we had thought, and that the Greed Syndrome is especially active on

Wall Street.

The Greed Syndrome is also operating within our system of law as surely as it is in the market place. We are expecting the courts to catch us up on a generation of ethical inattention, and finding they are ill-equipped to do so. There is a new climate within the legal system which lends itself to the escalation of greed and makes it possible to sue anybody for almost anything. Fault is no longer an important consideration, but rather who has the deepest pocket. A new book by Peter Huber, *Liability: the Legal Revolution and Its Consequences*, recently reviewed by Vincent Carroll, a nationally syndicated columnist, should, in his words, "convince all but the sleekest tort attorney that something is grossly wrong."

The problem comes from many sources, but lawyers seem to be especially responsible. The new attitude toward the law as a business, coupled with the general climate of greed within the nation, has produced a firestorm within the legal profession. The explosion of litigation, the escalation of the number of lawyers, the size of the awards, the rash of frivolous suits, all reflect our current hedonism. What we are witnessing is the prostitution of the American dream to the acquisition of quick and extravagant wealth.

Justice in the courts is in a strange kind of legal strait-jacket, with the primary concern directed to the tactics of law rather than the ideologies and strategies of justice. At the heart of this, as of all other symptoms of the Greed Syndrome, lies atheism and its counterpart, an exalted self-interest. This excessive individualism has led to a widespread aversion to personal responsibility, to restraint and punishment, and to a narrowing of our concerns to ourselves and those immediately related to us. There are many efforts within the legal profession to rectify injustices, past and present, but these are weakened by our long inattention to the ethical strategies of justice and to what a Biblical perspective might call a distortion of the entire process. A common observation is that technology has been running ahead of our understanding of what is moral and right.

The situation within the medical profession is a particularly painful example of the operation of the Greed Syndrome. The mentality of many doctors has changed with regard to their traditional idealism. The public has been led to expect more from medicine than is fair and realistic. Along with breakthroughs in science have gone a host of ethical problems for which we are not prepared. Unscrupulous patients, doctors, lawyers and insurance companies are taking advantage of this situation to get rich, and so threatening to destroy the medical profession as we know it.

We are living in the third generation of post-World War II affluence where we take this, not as a privilege, but as our right. This has led us to expect the best, to demand recompense for any inconvenience, to assume that doctors must be perfect. There is a widespread belief that we have a right to a life free of suffering. The common response is to sue if we don't get it. From a Biblical standpoint, all this identifies a serious ethical immaturity and a desperate need for a new sense of God's justice and sovereignty.

The insurance industry stands in the vortex of this whirlwind of greed. The universality of insurance and the vast wealth it represents have inevitably prompted people to take advantage of this situation, both outside and within the industry. The insurance mentality has created a substitute for faith, enhanced our fears and made us vulnerable to an artificially created demand for safety and the absence of risk beyond the bounds of reason or possibility.

The liability crisis is a two-way battle between defendants and plaintiffs, between lawyers and insurance companies. It extends throughout the whole economy and reveals a series of consistent patterns, whether within industry, Wall Street, the law, medicine or the insurance industry: vast sums of available cash, the escalation of greed from without and within, the surge of dishonesty, bizarre behavior, unrealistic expectations, the explosion of profits and costs, with the rich getting richer and the poor getting poorer, with collusion and selfishness threatening the health of the nation and the very existence of whatever profession. Along with these symptoms have also gone strenuous efforts to meet the various crises with mostly short-term, tactical solutions. There has been a surprisingly widespread recognition that excessive greed is operating and that we desperately need an effective ethic; but this is accompanied by a general lack of understanding of what this might mean.

From this study have come many insights that tell a consistent story. These speak at every point to the ethical breakdown within the American economy. They are presented here as workable tools for making ethical decisions. The higher pragmatism of the Bible is that when all the elements of God's sovereignty and justice are present, then things really, effectively, eternally work. The tactics that implement this ethic are to be found in the application to the social scene of the Apostle Paul's concept of maturity in love. The bottom line is an expression of hope and optimism which finds its particular justification in an ethic based upon the revelation of the God who transcends every age and condition of men and women.

Chapter 2

I Want to Be Rich

The evening news is over. It is time for "The Wheel of Fortune," one of the most popular programs on American TV. Amidst the whirring of a gigantic roulette wheel and the ecstatic response of the audience, we are treated to the vision of a beautiful woman, an elaborately colorful stage full of exotic prizes, and a panel of nervous players whipped to an expectant frenzy by their anticipation of receiving what every American must surely desire, an overflowing cornucopia of consumer goods. We are a nation of consumers. At least, that is what we are conceived to be by those who are paid to know.

Another scene claims our attention. The meeting has the appearance of an old time evangelistic service, with catchy songs, fervent testimonials and fiery sermons all dedicated to helping the overflowing and enthusiastic audience sell Nutralite, cosmetics and a wide variety of other products dedicated to making our bodies the healthiest and our homes the cleanest in the world. It is an Amway rally, perhaps history's classic example of evangelical consumerism bordering on cultism. It is one of the biggest marketing operations in the country, doing over a billion dollars in sales in its peak year, 1982. One has to purchase tickets for these rallies, the sale of which, along with motivational tapes and books, has netted one distributor, Dexter Yeager, about two thirds of his reported

$1.5 million annual income.

The plan is for one distributor to recruit another. At its peak, this amounted to 50,000 new applications per month. More recently, this is reported to be down to only 20,000. The most stable income, estimated from 30 to 60 per cent, seems to come from pressuring distributor recruits to purchase large amounts of these products themselves, and then from the selling of distributorships to an endless line of other recruits. This can be illegal and one thing that has plagued this enterprise is the actions of some distributors in what is called pyramiding, or "black hat." Each new recruit pays his or her distributor-recruiter a commission on their recruits. These in turn push their recruits to purchase large amounts of Amway goods, including tickets to motivational rallies. Although multi-millionaire co-founders Jay Van Andel and Richard DeVos have more recently tried to clean house, they continue to be plagued by this pyramiding activity within their ranks, as well as by a variety of charges, from improper marketing methods to Canadian customs fraud. (*Time*, Nov. 29, '82, 63) Despite these problems, Amway continues to be one of the largest direct-selling businesses in the country, second only to Avon. Although its business has declined since 1982, it is still very strong, and the company has moved into a diversity of other fields, like broadcasting and hotel ownership.

Not only does Amway illustrate the extent of the consumer mentality in America, but even more importantly the determination of many people to get rich as quickly as possible. As an article in *Broadcasting* magazine (Sept. 10, '84, 40) put it, commenting on the Amway phenomenon, "it is in the heart of people who like to get ahead...who have been up against the limits of their ability in the economic system. They are frustrated and seek a new way." And so Amway has tapped into this mood of frustration and produced a gusher of evangelical consumerism.

A less gargantuan but equally evangelical consumer enterprise is that of the Herbalife Corporation. Since its inception in 1982, the company has grown rapidly under the leadership of its young executive officer, Mark Hughes. According to Roy J. Harris Jr., staff reporter of *The Wall Street Journal*, its wholesale operations totaled $250 million in 1985, and retail sales by its distributors were about twice that amount. It, too, has had its problems. The State of California charged Herbalife International, Inc. with making false claims in promoting its wholesale line of nutritional aids and weight-loss products. One slim and trim product, Formula No. 2, is presented as helpful for more than 75 maladies, including balding, chicken pox and "female complaints."

This civil suit also charged that Herbalife is an illegal endless chain marketing system, where participants pay their recruiters to belong, and these in turn pass a percentage of this along the chain above them. According to Harris, this company claims to have restrained its extravagant advertising and instituted safeguards to prevent such pyramiding among its 700,000 distributors. Again, there seems to be an enormous response to this, another classic example of evangelical consumerism.

A Very Exclusive Club

Behind these more superficial symptoms of America's determination to get rich lies the real wealth of such multimillionaires as Merv Griffin who owned "The Wheel of Fortune" program or billionaires like the Cox sisters, whose empire includes the TV program, "Lifestyles of the Rich and Famous." These are the cheerleaders of this game. Its first string is idolized each year in *Forbes* magazine in a list of the 400 richest people in America, including Amway's Richard DeVos and Jay Van Andel.

"It has been a splendid year for billionaires" is the way *Forbes* begins its fifth annual edition of the *Forbes* Four Hundred. (Oct. 27, '86, 106) "Wealth in ten digits has been identified for 26 persons (in 1986), nearly double last year's tally." The minimum net worth of this list jumped $22 billion to

$156 billion in one year. The prerequisite for inclusion in this exclusive company increased $30 million, to $180 million, with "only a handful getting in that cheap." With the aid of the driving dynamic of Wall Street, ten of America's great fortunes at least doubled in 1986. The update for 1987 lists 49 billionaires, again almost double the previous year.

The Year of the Yuppie (Young Urban Professional)

This is the way *Newsweek* magazine headlined its classic cover story of December, 1984, highlighting what is one of the most visible illustrations of this fixation on wealth. Using as a working definition an income of $40,000 or more from a professional or management job, the California think-tank, SRI International, concluded that there were 4 million Americans between 25 and 39 who fit that description. *The Yuppie Handbook*, a tongue-in-cheek description of Yuppiehood, defines this group as persons of either sex who meet the following criteria: 1) resides in or near one of the major cities, 2) claims to be between the ages of 25 and 45, 3) lives on aspirations of glory, prestige, recognition, fame, social status, power, money, or any and all combinations of the above. According to *Newsweek*, the Yuppies are apparently convinced that money is the "root of all good."

Charles Colson, in *Christianity Today*, characterizes Yuppiedom in the view of the director of public service at an Atlanta TV station: "I've started to live the American dream. I want a business. I want to be rich. I want to have more money than I can spend. I want a Jaguar and maybe a quarter-of-a-million dollar house." The managing editor of *Money* magazine sums up that study's conclusion—what the Yuppies have discovered is nothing less than a new plane of "transcendental acquisition" in which the perfection of their possessions enables them to rise above "the messy turmoil of their emotional lives."

For those of us who agonized with the generation of the

1960s, with its Hippies, Yippies, and mostly just sensitive kids who were striking out at what they felt to be an inadequate older generation, this new movement is a fascinating, if partial, answer to a question often asked in that former generation. Where will all this passion and idealism go when the flower children have run out of flowers and the civil rights and anti-Vietnam enthusiasm has run out of gas? One answer is that this enthusiasm and idealism is still there; but instead of tackling the problems of the world, along with some concern for South Africa and Nicaragua, this generation has a more modest agenda: to address itself to the needs of individuals, the poor, the deviant, the oppressed, the aged. With those whose commitments are rather narrow, this gets translated into serving their own personal lives in the mood of radical individualism to which Robert Bellah refers. As *Newsweek* puts it, "much of the energy and optimism and passion of the '60s seems to have been turned inward, on lives, careers, apartments and dinners."

But it is much more complicated than that. There is a new generation gap that separates these Yuppies, some of whom were born in the '60s, from their parents as well as from their peers. In many ways, these are the opposite of what we used to call "the Now Generation." In the '60s they wore ragged jeans. Today, these wear designer jeans and pin-striped suits. They rejected the system and its affluence. These exploit the system and make affluence their top priority. They lived in rural communes or urban slums. These live in renovated lofts in the inner city. They abused their bodies with drugs until the Haight Asbury district in San Francisco was a disaster area. These are committed to health spas and jogging, or to a more sophisticated line of drugs. They were into the simple life and nature foods, these live in a complicated fast track and are dedicated to snails in mignonette sauce and hickory-smoked partridge.

But for all the differences, they are in many ways the same. Outwardly appearing as their parents wanted them to do, with haircuts, expensive clothing and a responsible job; they are really domesticated rebels taking the suburban values of their parents, of money, work, career, consumption, alcohol, sex and infidelity and turning these into a fine art. They are pursuing their view of the American dream with a vengeance. The more they do, the more they begin to appear as a mirror image of their counterparts of the 1960s. While accepting the superficial values of their parents, they are equally impatient with the past, radically individualistic and dedicated to self-realization. Rejecting any absolute standards that go beyond the individual or their particular set, they are suspicious of marital fidelity or anything that curtails sexual freedom. And they have little interest in religion or the organized church.

There is passion here, and some in this fast lane are no doubt both religious, idealistic and concerned for others. Generalizations are, of course, inadequate, but the picture seems to be that for most of this Yuppie sector of society, the social idealism of the '60s has been diverted into becoming rich as rapidly as possible. One cannot help but be aware that one of the most popular college majors has become that of business economics. In itself, this is neither good nor bad; many of the young people I know going into business continue to do so with a concern for religious and ethical values. But the tug toward evangelical consumerism is very strong and the temptation to shelve one's values in favor of the fast track is enormous. Charles Colson reports an incident at a car-rental establishment where a man ahead of him in line was loudly complaining that he had ordered a black Lincoln Continental, but the agency was trying to rent him a white one. "I'm going someplace where everyone will be driving a black car," he complained loudly. As he turned away in disgust, Colson saw emblazoned across his shirt a motto that put the whole matter into perspective: "The one who dies with the most toys wins."

Yuppie Religion

The strength and vitality of a movement can often be measured by the effect it has on religion. One of the most dramatic

illustrations comes from La Jolla, California, in the person of
Terry Cole-Whittaker. Author, lecturer, founder of Cole-
Whittaker Ministries, she has been pastor of what is sometimes
called the Yuppie church. This includes classes, seminars,
workshops, booklets, a newsletter, newspaper, phone-counsel-
ing, audio-tapes and nationwide television programs. Her
book, *How to Have More in a Have Not World*, is a good
summary of the Yuppie philosophy on the part of this attractive Christian minister who identifies with the evangelical consumer mentality and attempts to make it Christian. She
summarizes her message as "having all you truly desire within
a context or a framework of self-fulfillment and satisfaction."
Concerned that we all have both wealth and God, she tries to
help people find wholeness in realizing their spiritual potential
as they use their talents to transform the lives of other people.
She recognizes that money can be a problem, so she stresses
the need to learn and obey what she calls the unwritten laws of
life while practicing above all else the rule of love.

This is an attempt to Christianize contemporary hedonism.
The popularity of her program testifies not only to her elo-
quence, but to the consumer mentality we are examining. The
danger here is that of getting trapped in the very consumerism
one is trying to baptize. What she has done is re-write Christian theology in a Yuppie image and so produce a hyped-up
version of an ancient heresy called Pelagianism. According to
Pelagius, a fourth century British theologian, we can raise ourselves by our own moral bootstraps without any real depend-
ence on the grace of God. For Cole-Whittaker, despite her
occasional references, God is not really necessary except as an
impersonal force to be used in "having all you desire, within a
context of self-fulfillment and satisfaction." Jesus Christ seems
to play little part in her thinking and his teaching about the
kingdom of God is entirely absent. For her, "love is the fundamental, absolute truth of life. It is all there is." And so the
God of Moses and Isaiah, of Jesus and Paul, whose justice
includes both love and wrath, both command and the freedom
to disobey, is exchanged for a kind of divinized eros. This

gospel of self-realization rejects any self-denial or any compulsion to do what one does not want to do. It thus creates many misconceptions about the Christian ethic and ultimately invalidates Cole-Whittaker's concern that people take seriously these "unwritten laws of life" which she doesn't bother to spell out.

This is a good illustration of Bellah's analysis of the current mood of radical individualism, pluralism and self-actualization, finding its way into the practice of the Christian religion. At points, it makes pretty good psychology and appears to be a promising beginning for a bridge across the chasm between the Yuppie mentality and the Christian faith. But it cannot be called a Christian statement. It sounds very much like a movement in the first several Christian centuries called Gnosticism in which early Christian thinkers tried to combine Christian ideas with a hodge-podge of concepts from Greek, Syrian and Egyptian philosophy and religion. This produced a variety of exotic sects which sprang up like the wildflowers of Spring and died as quickly, usually with the passing of their charismatic founders. It is instructive to find an acknowledgment of Cole-Whittaker's indebtedness to "the gnostics" at the beginning of her book.

Is the Greed Syndrome operating here? It seems to be in this creative attempt to re-write Christian theology to fit the prevailing desire to "have more." There is a great danger in getting quite so close to the god "mammon." We tend to become its servants without knowing it. When the Gospel gets so slick and packaged in the trappings of a consumer society, it tends to take on some of the mentality of that society. At this point, the Greed Syndrome has begun to operate.

This is especially prevalent among the more flamboyant evangelists of this generation who often begin with a prophetic call from God and a dedication to the things of the Spirit, but who get caught up in the TV mentality of the "rich and the famous," and succumb to the temptations of wealth, power and adulation. They fly too high, over-extend their mission, and the prophetic vision becomes confused with wealth and delusions of grandeur. At this point, we become aware of the strident plea for money, and sometimes an extravagant lifestyle, which seems to have little similarity to God's word as revealed in the humble carpenter of Nazareth they all claim to follow. The Greed Syndrome operates subtly and pervasively within our American culture. It is especially contagious at the points of our contact with power, popularity and wealth.

The Poverty of Affluence

Our wealth has brought many great benefits, but the fall-out has been awesome. Much that we had thought beneficial is now threatening to destroy us. The internal combustion engine, heralded as one of the greatest breakthroughs in the history of industrialization, is now choking our cities and furthering the destruction of the ozone layer. The development of mass production, one of the greatest sources of our affluence, has produced the kind of technological sickness described by Toffler in his book, *Future Shock*, or Reich in *The Greening of America*. Our affluence has created the threat of ecological disaster. It has inundated us with the results of the demand for constantly increasing consumption. It has produced violent polarization in homes and schools, and in our economy. We are not as certain as we used to be about the benefits of such great affluence.

One aspect of the Greed Syndrome comes from the interaction of these two poles of our affluence. On the one hand are those persons of great wealth who operate within a climate of profits far outstripping anything dreamed of by John D. Rockefeller, Jay Gould or Commodore Vanderbilt in the halcyon days following the Civil War, before the financial panic of the 1870s. Making large sums of money has become for many today a gigantic game of Monopoly where controlling markets and pushing money about is done for the sheer fun of it. The lure of pleasure, power and prestige that goes with the game is an intoxicating mixture. The *Forbes* 400, along with all those who almost meet these standards, represent an exotic and exciting way of life. The push toward evangelical consumerism is understandable.

On the other hand, the temptation to the excesses of greed comes strongly out of the agony of frustration among the poor, and the not quite successful, whose lives are lived out just above or below the official poverty line. Two-job families, moonlighting, evangelical consumer programs, reflect the widespread difficulty in making ends meet. There is also the envy of those in the outside lane who would like to be tearing along with others in the fast track. The lack of concern for the details of honesty and strict compliance with the law is one symptom of this Greed Syndrome. It is easier to obey the law when you can pay your bills; but this temptation also affects some in that other economic stratum. We are all ultimately cut from the same cloth.

It is not really so strange that, with the extravagant affluence of this age, we also have a pathetically bizarre rash of poverty. Even America must chasten its romantic 19th century dreams of unlimited abundance. If some gobble up more than is consistent with economic justice, then others must starve. Hunger and affluence, Steinbeck's *Grapes of Wrath* and the TV *Dallas*, are at war with one another today; this tension is one of the major sources of what I am calling the Greed Syndrome.

What Does the Bible Say?

The Hebrew-Christian ethic has always been the primary defense against the escalation of greed in this country. It has done so by an unrelenting challenge to two attitudes absolutely basic to the Greed Syndrome: the primacy of material values and the autonomy of human economic activity. The prophet Micah summarized the Old Testament ethic: "What does the Lord require of you but to do justice, love mercy and walk humbly with your God?" (6:8) Jesus echoed the same theme in a summary statement within the Sermon on the Mount: "Seek first the Kingdom of God and his righteousness." More exactly, both Old and New Testament are in agreement in applying this ethic to the economic scene: "You cannot serve God and Mammon." (Matt. 6:24) The emphasis here is on the word "serve," as Jesus makes clear in Luke 16:13: "No servant can serve two masters; for either he will hate the one and love the other, or he will be devoted to one and despise the other."

In the Old Testament there are four major sources of ethical instruction: the Covenant code (Exodus 20:22-23:33), the books of the prophets, the book of Deuteronomy and the Holiness code in Leviticus 11-26. Some of these rules are so specifically directed to the concerns of the ancient middle eastern Semitic culture that they have been ignored either by Hebrews, or Christians or both. But the basic thrust of this ethic remains as a common core of Hebrew-Christian belief. It is this which has been the source of direction and restraint for the American economy since the days of the Spanish explorers and the Pilgrim fathers and mothers.

The Earth Is the Lord's

The Hebrew-Christian thinking about any subject always begins with the person and nature of God. So America in applying this ethic has seen itself as a "nation under God." This is a sovereign God of Justice who is Lord of the earth, whose sovereignty is not to be taken lightly and whose justice is the ultimate, absolute standard for human behavior. The most fundamental ethical command of this tradition is to reflect in every area of our lives the nature of God. We are to do justice because God is a God of justice. We are to love mercy because God's justice is one of infinite love. We are to fear God because His wrath is an expression of his justice. We are required to do justice because his justice comes to us as a command. We are expected to make responsible choices because God's justice gives us freedom to obey or disobey. It is within the interplay of love and wrath, of command and freedom, that the justice of God works itself out within the lives of men and women. When any one of these elements is missing, we have an unjust situation that will not work. Life works only God's way.

"Do Not Be Anxious"

Jesus inherited this ethical tradition and we see it reflected in his Sermon on the Mount as well as in his parables. "Do not be anxious about your life, what you shall eat...nor about your body, what you shall put on. Is not life more than food, and the body more than clothing...if God clothes the grass of the field...will he not much more clothe you?...but seek first his kingdom and his righteousness (justice), and all these things shall be yours as well." In the parable of the Pounds and Talents (Matt. 25:14-30), he expands on this theme by comparing his audiences to servants of a landowner who gives them money with which to trade and then returns and demands to know how responsibly they have handled his investment. In the parable of the Wicked Husbandmen (Mark 12:1-12), he modifies a similar parable of Isaiah (5:1-5), picturing his audience as servants in a vineyard refusing to render a responsible accounting for their stewardship. "I will tell you what I will do to my vineyard," said Isaiah. "I will remove its hedge, and it shall be devoured...he looked for justice, but behold bloodshed; for righteousness, but behold a cry." "What will the owner of the vineyard do?" said Jesus. "He will come and destroy the tenants and give the vineyard to others." The problem in all this is that men and women in their pride and ambition refuse to see their possessions as gifts of God, and themselves as stewards in his vineyard.

There Is Nothing Wrong With Economic Activity

Jesus, along with his Hebrew ethos, accepted the first century economic system and was sympathetically involved in it.

Only eight of his parables in the first three Gospels are not based on some analogy to the economic system. The kingdom of God is like a merchant in search of a pearl of great price (Matt. 13:45). It is like a farmer hiring laborers for his fields and agreeing to pay them the prevailing wage. (Matt. 20:1f.) It is like a field of growing grain (Matt. 13:24), or a king's household where the servants are called to account, and one is found who owes the king an enormous debt and is ordered to pay (Matt.18:23). Jesus seems to have accepted the right of the government to tax its citizens (Mk12:41; Matt.17:27), and he shows a surprising sympathy for tax collectors, eating with them (Matt. 9:10), defending them (Matt. 11:19; Lk. 15:l; Matt. 10:3), and calling one of them, Matthew, into his disciple band. (Matt. 9:10; 10:3; Lk.15:1) He even seems to have approved of the principle of usury, basing several parables on the right of a rich man to expect a return on his investment. (Matt. 25:14-30; Luke 19:11)

Jesus also accepted the principle of profit and drew one of his most common analogies to the life of the kingdom of God from the desire to make a profit on buying and selling (Matt. 13:45; Luke 7:41), on vineyards (Matt. 20:1-16), and fig trees (Luke 21:29), and on the productivity of servants within the household of a wealthy landowner. (Mark 13:33; Luke 12:42; 17:7) The distaste for economic activity so prevalent in the Middle Ages seems to have been a product of later social forces based on an inadequate understanding of the Bible. Before modern tools like concordances were developed for Bible study, really only in the last century, it was standard practice to lift selected passages out of context and use them as a basis for one's own ideas. Comprehensive Biblical study, and especially the application of the scientific methods of research, is a product of modern Western culture. So we are in a better position today to understand what the Bible is saying about these matters.

But Jesus Warned Against the Abuses of Wealth

In his discussion with the rich young man (Matt. 19:16-30), Jesus warned that it is hard for a rich man or woman to enter the kingdom of heaven; not because of some absolute prohibition against wealth, but because wealth, and especially great wealth, tends to command our allegiance and so stand in the way of primary allegiance to God. Actually, this passage assumes that some of the sons and daughters of the kingdom will be wealthy. "It is easier for a camel to go through the eye of a needle than for a rich man to enter the kingdom of God." (Mark 10:25) The "needle's eye" to which he referred was probably the kind of small inner door one can still see within the large wooden Jaffa gate on the Western edge of the Old City of Jerusalem. It would be difficult, but conceivable, for a camel to go through that door. Furthermore, he concludes this incident with the assurance that those who abandon mothers and fathers and lands, for his sake, will "receive a hundredfold now in this time, houses and mothers and children and lands ...and... eternal life." (Mark 10:30) There is the possibility of present reward for such dedication, but only as a by-product of a deeper commitment to the things of the Spirit.

Jesus was not against wealth *per se*. The predominant pattern in the Gospels is that he opposed vigorously the abuse of wealth, and this describes the basic symptoms of the Greed Syndrome. The most serious was allowing money to stand in the way of God, as with the rich young ruler. In his parable of the sower, the weeds which grew up to choke the seed of God's word are variously interpreted by him, including "the cares of the world and the delight in riches." (Mark 4:19) He warned against "covetousness," or greed, insisting that "a man's life does not consist in the abundance of his possessions" (Luke 12:15), and warned against allowing money to make one "anxious." (Matt. 6:25)

In the Parable of the Rich Fool, he condemned the man who built bigger barns to hold his produce, not because of the abundance of his harvest, but because wealth had become a

selfish accumulation for personal satisfaction, another symptom of the Greed Syndrome. "Soul, you have ample goods laid
up for many years; take your ease, eat, drink, be merry." Here
is the ultimate poverty of affluence: rich in goods, but not rich
toward God. "Fool! This night your soul is required of you; and
the things you have prepared, whose will they be?" (Luke
12:13-21) I Timothy echoed the same warning: "As for the rich
in this world, charge them not to be haughty, nor to set their
hopes on uncertain riches but on God who richly furnishes us
with everything to enjoy." (6:17)

Ostentatious substitute for genuine piety was another
abuse of wealth that Jesus was concerned to parody in those
around him. The story of the widow's mite (Mark 12:41-44) is
well known; the pompous Pharisee who bragged that he gave
"tithes of all that he possessed" is another caricature of the
self-righteousness of wealth. Jesus' response was to urge the
wealthy, the powerful and the religious to "give for alms those
things that are within." (Lk. 11:41) "When you give alms,
sound no trumpet...in the streets...that your alms may be in
secret, that your Father who sees in secret will reward you."
(Matt. 6:2-4)

Allowing money to corrupt morality and concern for
others is one of the most common problems of wealth and
symptoms of greed. The Covenant code in the book of Exodus
warns that we must not bear false witness against our neighbor,
nor "follow a multitude so as to pervert justice." (23:1-3) Jesus
criticized the Scribes and Pharisees that they "tithe mint and
rue and every herb, and neglect justice and the love of God."
(Luke 11:42) The way one acquires and then handles his or her
wealth is the pivot of the Hebrew-Christian ethic. At this point,
Moses and Jesus were very severe.

In two controversial passages, the author of Luke records
Jesus saying, "Woe unto you rich, for you have received your
consolation," and the author of James, "Come now, you rich,
weep and howl for the miseries that are coming upon you."
(5:1) When lifted out of context, these passages have been
used to place Jesus in radical opposition to all men and women

of wealth. This is unfortunate for it limits Jesus' sympathies in a way that a comprehensive examination of his teaching does not permit. It is clear from other indications in their books that Luke and the author of James seem to have had a strong bias against the rich and in favor of the poor. For example, where Matthew says, "Blessed are the poor in spirit," Luke has, "Blessed are you poor." (Matt. 5:3; Luke 6:20) But to attribute such a bias to Jesus does both Jesus and persons of wealth a grave injustice. His Gospel was never so doctrinaire in rejecting any class of society. If one considers this warning in the light of all Jesus is recorded as saying on this subject, I would say that it reflects not a bias against wealth itself, but a vigorous condemnation of those who abuse their abilities and the gifts of God's abundance.

Prostitution Is Its Name

While accepting the validity of wealth and the necessity of the profit motive, the Hebrew-Christian ethic has always insisted on the need for restraints on greed. The profit motive is out of control when that which is productive as a means to an end becomes destructive as an end in itself. Prostitution is always the misuse of some human function when it becomes not a service to persons or society, but merely something to play with. This could be sex or food or work or wealth or power. When any of the legitimate functions of life become ends in themselves so that they crowd out the worship of God, then they become self-destructive. This is the danger of the frantic pursuit of money which characterizes a large portion of American society. Christian theology places our property, wealth and time under the sovereignty of God. He is the lord of the earth. The amount of things we own, the way we get them and the use to which we put them are all regulated, whether we like it or not, by the justice of God. We are reminded by this Hebrew-Christian tradition that God calls us to be stewards of our wealth. What this means is to recognize that all we are and do stands under the judgment of God.

Is Capitalism an Immoral System?

The current economic scene is driving us to reconsider our basic beliefs about capitalism and about morality itself. In a nation describing itself as being "under God," the question is, what does this mean in terms of the economy? The two historic alternatives have been the economics of Adam Smith, based on individual self-interest operating through a competitive free market, and various forms of socialism which are based upon the primary concern for individuals and society, the restraint of self-interest and the discouraging or prohibiting of competition. From each according to his ability, to each according to his need, is the watchword of socialism, an idea which had its roots in the New Testament, but was later preempted by Karl Marx.

This continuing debate has been enlivened by the emergence of what *Harper's* "Forum" recently referred to as "a new school of conservative advocates who assert the superior morality of capitalism over all other economic systems." There are others in this discussion, like Lewis Lapham, editor of *Harper's* magazine, who see no reason for making this an ethical discussion at all. But surely this is nonsense. By definition, ethics deals with the ways we act in our ethos; we will act one way or another, whether we admit it or not. Moral chaos itself is a system of ethics. To say that the way we act is not a matter of ethical concern is to say it does not matter how we act. This is exactly the problem. One of our greatest needs is to bring the ethical state of our nation into conscious discussion.

In an ethical comparison of capitalism and socialism, there are several key issues that sharpen the differences:

l) Perhaps the most fundamental is whether the economy should be based upon self-interest, as Adam Smith advocated in *The Wealth of Nations*, or upon the interest of the total group, as urged by Karl Marx in *Das Kapital*. The ever-present danger for capitalism is the tendency toward greed, which is self-interest out of control. With socialism, the danger is apathy and the loss of incentive which comes from not recognizing the natural and potentially healthy desire of men and women to improve themselves.

2) Another fundamental issue is whether this is to be a free economy as proposed by Adam Smith or a more planned and tightly controlled one which is the tendency of socialism. The Christians discovered in the first century, with the dishonesty of Ananias and Saphira, that in that early communal experiment everyone is not going to play the game (Acts 5), and so force is almost always necessary to restrain the human ego.

3) The capitalist economy, it is said, offers the most efficient system, based as it is on the self-interested necessity for survival. The creative dynamism, the huge profits available in a capitalist economy as contrasted with the more radically socialist countries, are becoming so apparent that even China, and now Russia are moving subtly toward the use of the profit motive as an incentive to get their economies out of the doldrums. On the other hand, the impersonal efficiency of capitalism is contrasted with the self-conscious concern for persons within socialist economies. These aim to correct the inequalities, the poverty, the loss of dignity, the destruction of families which is the constant danger within capitalism.

4) In recent years, a third way has been emerging which is a blending of the two systems. America is no longer capitalist in the sense defined by Adam Smith in the eighteenth century. We are too much aware of the squalor of the sweat shops of the early industrial revolution, the excesses of what Josephson called the "Robber Barons" of the nineteenth century, and the Great Depression of the 1930s. The successes of the New Deal, the economic theories of John Maynard Keynes and a host of revisionists since World War II, have brought Democrats and Republicans closer and closer together in what some social philosophers like Robert Benne call "Democratic Capitalism."

What Are the Deeper Issues?

Efficiency and ethics seem to summarize the concerns that have caused this subtle but profound shifting of our economy. The issues are still with us and the Greed Syndrome drives us to consider more deeply what the Hebrew-Christian ethic says about the morality of democratic capitalism. I find five major principles in our traditional ethical base which define the issues and point to some answers.

1) Systems can be unjust, but only men and women can be evil. This is an important theological-ethical distinction that will inform our analysis of the Greed Syndrome. Injustice can be expressed by a nation or an economy, and it is conceivable that some systems lend themselves more to injustice than to justice; but ultimately evil is a personal matter. It is the "unforgivable sin" which is the rejection of the Spirit of God from our personal lives. (Mark 3:29; Cf. *RPG*-93) In the Gospels, for example, Jesus excoriates his contemporaries for the injustice of their social policies (Luke 11:42), but he is never recorded using the word *poneros* (evil) for anything except persons. The closest he came was calling his an "evil generation" (Matt. 12:45); but this collective evil is merely a description of a group of evil individuals. (Matt. 13:38;18:32 etc.) What this says is that it is they, individually and collectively, not the system they operate under, who are what the Bible would call evil.

The practical issue involved here is that exclusively systemic thinking usually creates two problems:

a) If we concentrate in our ethical concerns solely or even primarily on society and its structures, systems, programs and laws, we have missed the important personal dimension to the problem. Given the propensity of some systems to injustice, the heart of injustice is not any particular system but an individual human psyche rebelling against God.

b) The systemic approach is in danger of what I call "the group fallacy." That is, we tend to personify groups, structures and systems, attributing to them the evil that is properly to be identified within the human soul. A group is an abstraction, a collection of individuals bound together by some need or set of beliefs that is constantly forming and dissolving. To personify social groupings lends itself to the objectification of evil where we demonize "the military-industrial complex" or communism as "the evil empire," or the U.S. as "the great Satan" or capitalism as an "evil" system. What this all suggests is that we need to pay attention to the justice or injustice of our systems. They are all a mixed bag, but until we get into the personal, individual dimension of the group, we will not have grappled with the driving, erotic heart of the matter and the essential focal point of evil.

2) This suggests that there is no Christian economic system, but only Christians, or godly men and women of whatever formal affiliation, operating within any given system. Economies can contain elements which tend toward ethical abuse and some systems seem more prone to injustice than others. Capitalism tends toward the abuse of freedom and the promotion of greed. Communism tends toward repression and the stifling of creativity. But given a genuine concern for justice, and with men and women committed to the sovereignty of God, it is my guess that most economic systems can be made to work: how *well* is a complicated technical question beyond the scope of this ethical analysis.

3) Survival, self-interest, the profit motive, the desire to get ahead, the desire to express oneself creatively, even aggressively, what the ancient Greeks called *eros*, is not in and of itself evil. The key to a Christian *eros* is whether or not it accepts the sovereignty of God and expresses his justice.

4) The Hebrew-Christian ethic is more concerned with persons than it is with profits. It is this which leads men like Czechoslovakian theologian Milan Opocensky to insist that socialism is a more Christian economic system. When capitalism grinds up men and women in its efficient machine, then one must admit that this is true. What I will try to show, however, is that this is not the inevitable product of the capitalist system, but only of that system out of touch with the ethical and religious factors necessary to its success.

5) Finally, the Hebrew-Christian ethic that has sustained the best in our American economy through the years places God and others ahead of self. It is not a choice of either-or, but a matter of priorities. "Seek first the kingdom of God and his justice." That is the most fundamental of all Hebrew and Christian ethical guidelines. When Jesus says "deny yourself," or "lose your life to find it," he is not advocating asceticism or suicide or self-rejection in its modern psychological sense. He is telling us to put our priorities in order: to love God first, and then to love others, and finally to love ourselves. (Mark 12:28-34)

Both Testaments remind us that we cannot put both God and money first in our lives. There is a great danger that the evangelical consumerism we have been examining is being shipwrecked against this great ethical headland. The answer I will be proposing throughout this book is that we will resolve this dilemma neither by some kind of rejection of ourselves or our economy, nor by re-writing Christianity in the image of Mammon. We will resolve it rather in the way the Bible tells us to do, by redeeming and transforming Mammon in the service of God.

Chapter 3

I Want More

Mammon is a god which insists on being a servant of none but itself. The concern for wealth comes to a much more universal focus in the determination of salary. Here we see the same forces at work as we do in the accumulation of wealth: the extension of the Greed Syndrome into the work ethic of America.

The Salary Explosion

Salaries have gone through the roof. At least, the top salaries have. This has created an imbalance in our salary structure that is both a symptom and a cause of the Greed Syndrome. The 1987 Roman Catholic Bishops' Pastoral, *Economic Justice for All, Catholic Social Teaching and the U.S. Economy*, reports that men and women of all classes and political persuasions share a common misgiving that in recent years something in the economy has drastically changed. One element of this is that the rich seem to be getting richer and the poor getting poorer. This comes to special focus in the radical disparity within the salary structure of our nations. It is one of the principal symptoms and fuels of the Greed Syndrome. We are involved in a frantic salary game where the players are most of us and the stars receive salaries almost beyond belief.

The Rich are Getting Richer

The highest salaries go to those most skilled in the making
or manipulation of money. *Financial World* (July 14, '87, 30f)
lists the top 100 salaries of those actively related to Wall Street
as ranging annually from $3 million to $100 million in 1986,
escalating to $125 million in 1987. Many have written about
the unreality of newly graduated MBAs from the top business
schools earning $100,000 in their first year (*Financial World*,
July 22, '86, 15). According to a *Newsweek* survey (May 26, '86,
471), it is not uncommon for some to earn over a million a year
within 3 to 10 years if they happen to get on the right track.
Since the Wall Street crash in 1987, with a reported 35,000 jobs
lost as a result, this has probably changed; but with major
banks pushing aggressively into investment banking, Wall
Street leaders continue to expect "astronomical compensation." This is despite the fact that the one with the top salary
for 1987, Ivan Boesky, was subsequently indicted by the SEC
and sentenced to three years in prison for insider trading.

According to *Fortune* magazine, the average salary of the
chief executive officers of our major corporations is $400,000.
A more recent update by the management consulting firm of
Towers, Perrin, Forster & Crosby reports that the median total
cash compensation for chief executives in 1987 passed the $1
million mark for the first time, with Lee Iacocca, president of
Chrysler Motors, leading the field at $17.9 million. Rick
Gladstone, AP business writer, charges that American executives receive the highest pay of any industrialized democracy,
rising faster than inflation, corporate profits or worker wages.
This ought to be enough; but the same demand for more seems
to be operating within these exalted ranks. A case in point
surrounds the ouster of H. Ross Perot as a director of General
Motors. Perot was forced to resign in a controversial $700
million stock buyout aimed at stopping his criticism of the

management of this, the world's largest corporation and car maker. At a time when GM was suffering from an earnings decline and resulting large layoffs and when its profitability and competitiveness were slipping seriously, Perot was highly critical of the management for proposing large executive bonuses. Speaking to reporters before an address at the Detroit Economic Club, Perot said he would vote against the proposed bonuses if the company was not going to be in a position to pay profit-sharing to hourly workers. He is quoted saying that "in war you feed the troops before you feed the officers." (Reuters, '87) This is noble sentiment, but one wonders about the $700 million.

Salary fever has turned up with particular vigor in the field of sports where the stars seem to revolve in their own orbit. *Sports Illustrated* (March, '86) reports that between 1974 and 1985 the average salary among baseball players rose from $40,819 to $329,408, with the highest salary escalating from Dick Allen's $225,000 in 1974 to Mike Schmidt's $2,130,000 in 1985. In 1985 the average salary for the top 32 players was $1,279,687. At least 36 players were expected to make more than $1 million, compared with 22 in 1984. To this one must, of course, add bonuses and other incentive clauses. And the ante continues to rise with arbitration suits and the weapon of free agency luring more and more players to demand a larger share of the take.

And so the fever has spread to professional football with the 1987 strike that threw the league standings into a turmoil and gave a lot of surprised second stringers a chance at the big time. The issue was ostensibly that of free agency; but if the baseball experience is any indication, the real issue was one of creating the climate wherein football players could get their salaries up to the level of those in baseball. As Ron Mix, former tackle and Hall of Famer complained in *Sports Illustrated* (Oct. '87), their counterparts in baseball earn about twice the football players' $230,000 a year and several times their pension benefits.

The logic on the player's side is that the life of a football player is filled with pain and injury, with a professional career potential of 3.5 years and a life expectancy of 55 years. For this they feel they should be compensated in ways that provide them with lifetime support. But in the strike they overplayed their hand and the NFL's image was badly damaged. In a Dallas *Times Herald* telephone poll conducted the first day of the strike, 82 per cent of the respondents supported the NFL owners. The former player who was to broadcast the Browns game (Oct. 26), when interviewed by Wilma Smith, Cleveland TV, although sympathetic with the union, was badly disillusioned. He felt the players had acted irresponsibly and feared this kind of thing could destroy the union. Very little was gained by the strike. Relationships within the clubs were severely strained and the salary lost could probably never be made up. One clear result was the loss of faith in the players by a disgruntled public who, however unfairly, as one national commentator put it, interpreted this as a bunch of multi-millionaires sitting around striking for more money. Greed is not a popular thing, wherever it is found.

Unions are coming under increasing criticism for their part in fueling the Greed Syndrome. Born in an era where workers were brutally exploited and salaries could not support their families, the union movement has done a historic job of raising the position of workers to one of dignity and economic viability. But success has also fueled the Greed Syndrome with the inordinate escalation of salary demands and frequent corruption within the leadership. In recent years, union power has grown to the point where strikes or the threat of strikes have pushed companies over the edge of bankruptcy, driven them out of the major industrial cities into areas of non-union dominance, or forced them out of the country entirely. A new phenomenon which will bear watching is the incursion into American business of a foreign company, like the new Mitsubishi auto industry, whose work philosophy and economic survival is based upon recruiting non-union workers. The initial idealism of the union movement has been lost in the escalating demands for more salary, more benefits, more job security to the extent that the operation of the Greed Syndrome is destroying American unions.

"Born into wealth, Donald Trump wants more," was the headline of an article from the Associated Press by Rick Hampson. Operator of four casinos, five hotels, and two skating rinks, Trump is completing a high-rise condominium in Palm Beach, and planning the world's tallest building in Manhattan. City residents complain that this would cast a winter shadow a mile and a half long and swamp their already overcrowded streets. (*Time*, Nov. 30, '87) At 41, Trump claims to have $550 million in ready cash and appears to control $1 billion in mortgageable real estate. His philosophy well describes the Greed Syndrome where winning is everything. "Man is the most vicious of animals, and life is a series of battles ending in defeat or victory. You can't let people make a sucker out of you." (*Mansfield News Journal*, Oct 25, '87) But in his drive for more and more, Trump seems to be treading the boundary between what is legal and what is ethical. According to *FTC: Watch*, a biweekly newsletter that reports on the Federal Trade Commission, the agency asked the Justice Department to prosecute Trump for illegal use of what is called a "parking agreement," whereby a corporate raider uses a third party to help him secretly amass shares in a takeover target in violation of federal law. Trump admitted this, but denied it was illegal. (*Time*, Nov. 30, '87, 67)

From Prophet To Priest

We seem to be suckered in every area, even that of religion. The most recent classic illustration is that of Jim and Tammy Bakker. The news media labeled this as a sex case. More properly, it was not sex but greed that lay at the heart of this matter. Born the son of a piston ring machinist, Bakker describes himself in his autobiography, *Move That Mountain*, as one raised in poverty. Ordained a minister by the Assemblies of God, in the course of his traveling evangelistic ministry, Bakker developed a theology that unified the Christian Gospel with materialism and the promise of wealth and success as the rewards of piety.

The story of the rise and fall of the PTL club has been widely reported in the media. (*Time,* Aug. 3, '87) What has surfaced is a tale of Christian commitment, subverted by the temptations of fame and financial success, and perverted by a misunderstanding of Christian stewardship. Along with his boyish charm and religious commitment also apparently went a driving ambition to build bigger and bigger palaces for the Lord, and, incidentally, for himself and Tammy Faye. From his first Heritage Village TV studio in Charlotte, to Heritage USA, the 500 room Heritage Grand Hotel, the unfinished Heritage Towers, and his ultimate vision of a $100 million replica of London's Crystal Palace, there seemed to be no limit to his visions of grandeur.

The Bakkers' salary and compensation were equally grandiose, perhaps outdistancing anything ever seen in an American Christian ministry. The scandal broke with full fury in 1987 with the ouster of Bakker as head of PTL, and the painful attempts to unravel an impossibly chaotic financial situation. The subsequent managers of PTL estimated Bakker's salary to be $1.6 million in 1986. This included the discovery that PTL sold 120,000 "Lifetime Partnerships" for $1,000 each to families guaranteed free hotel lodging for a limited period each year in facilities so overbooked it was impossible to accommodate them all. After 15 months of investigation, Bakker was indicted on 24 counts of fraud and conspiracy. Thus it would seem that fraud was a partner to extravagance in this strange wedding of God and mammon. The prophet Jeremiah seems to be describing our present situation as well as his own with uncanny accuracy:

> "For from the least to the greatest of them,
>   every one is greedy for unjust gain;
>   and from prophet to priest,
>   every one deals falsely.

Therefore they shall fall among those who fall;
at the time that I punish them,
they shall be overthrown," says the Lord.

(Jer. 6:13,15)

And The Poor Are Getting Poorer

The special significance of these extreme case studies is the contrast they provide with the growing poverty in our nation. The opposite end of the spectrum is, of course, the increasing numbers living on the streets of our great cities, a poignant signal to the world that, for some, freedom in America means the freedom to starve. One of the best and most recent studies of poverty is found in the report of the U.S. Roman Catholic Bishops' Pastoral Letter: *Economic Justice for All*. This document is based upon the U.S. Department of Agriculture's assumption that in 1961 an average family spent one third of its income on food. By tripling the basic nutritional requirements of a family of three, it was determined that $7,938 was the boundary between poverty and a viable income. In 1960 there were 39,851,000 or 22 per cent of the population who lived in poverty according to that definition. Since then the figures have varied down and up, with a reduction to 11.1 per cent in 1973 and a rise to 15.2 per cent, or 35,266,000 in 1983.

More startling figures describe the situation of women and minorities, with poverty among blacks going from 41 per cent in 1960 to 35 per cent in 1983, and families headed by females from 49 per cent in 1960 to 35 per cent in 1983. The poor are most likely to be children under fifteen, women, blacks and Hispanics, even though the absolute majority of the poor are whites. Fifty percent of all black children under six live in poverty. In November of 1987, it was reported that one quarter of the population of New York City lives below the poverty level. "It is the grimness of poverty that troubles us more than any other problem," stated the blue ribboned "Commission of the Year 2,000" which had been studying New York's needs. (*Time*, Nov. 30, '87)

The Disparity Defines the Problem

There is a large base of poverty in this country, and the disparity between the poor and the wealthy is growing. The Bishops' Letter concludes that "The gap between rich and poor in our nation had increased during the last decade." (p. 51, f.n. 36) Subsequently, it became a major concern of the last presidential election. In 1984 the lowest 20 per cent of American families received only 4.7 per cent of the total national income, with the bottom 40 per cent receiving 15.7 per cent. Compared with this the top 20 per cent received 42.9 per cent of the total income, the highest share since 1948. It is this radical disparity more than anything else that raises ethical questions with regard to salary. Contrary to some expectations, the Olympian escalation of top salaries has not done much to raise the level of those at the bottom. If anything, it has probably compounded the problem. An NBC poll reported (10/18/88) that the rich are not as generous in giving time and money for the poor as are those in the middle and lower incomes.

The trickle-down theory is not working at the level of human concern. Wealth, greed and self-interest tend to go together. Whether this system stimulates the economy is a technical economics question. My impression is that whatever it does for the economy, its side effect is the radical disparity we have been examining.

Some would insist that there is only so much cash and property available in this game of monopoly. From that standpoint, the logic is clear. If some get more than their just share, then others must get less. The obscene disparity being described here supports this view. Ravi Batra, Professor of Economics at SMU, in a new book, *The Great Depression of 1990*, warns that every 60 years a great disparity in wealth triggers a depression. This disparity is not only a serious economic question, but, as Jeremiah reminds us, a profoundly ethical one as well and one of the prime symptoms of the Greed Syndrome.

What About All of Us in Between?

More representative of the total situation is a salary study derived from the relevant government documents. This is a highly varied, constantly changing picture, but there are some patterns that stand out. To begin with, the average annual earnings for non-supervisory workers vary from just above the poverty level to a comfortable wage approximating that of many of the higher-salaried professionals. Wages for laborers differ widely from job to job and county to county. In a 1986 survey, California wages varied from $4.50 to $48.00 per hour, with a skilled dock worker carpenter receiving a median $19.27, which comes to $36,998 for 48 weeks, with fringe benefits of approximately $25,000 annually. The average wage for the same length of time in that year for non-supervisory workers across the country was approximately $14,632 with the lowest on the California scale being $8,640 and the highest $92,160.

Professional and supervisory salaries are equally varied, but begin well above the poverty level. The following table gives a representative sample of annual salaries from the 1982 Census report. This, of course, is flawed because there is no way to account for all the benefits, bonuses and auxiliary income that comes with the particular profession. These figures represent the over-all average salary within what in some cases is a very wide range of differences. To compare adequately with the above California survey, one would need to compensate for the salary rise between '82 and the '88 census, and that story has not yet been told. Available figures point to an average rise in professional salaries during this period of approximately 24 per cent. The important thing for us is not the

absolute numbers, but the relative comparisons. I see no indication that this has substantially changed.

CEOs	$400,000
Physicians	$100,000
Attorneys	$43,900
Chemists	$37,000
Radio and TV announcers	$36,000
Accountants	$33,000
College, University teachers	$25,500
Bank Officers	$24,500
Secondary School teachers	$21,000
Police	$18,600
Protestant Ministers	$16,500

In the above, there are certain ethical observations one
might make with regard to the ways that salaries either reflect
or are out of step with our American system of values. The
most obvious is that professions dealing with money are the
highest paid. The next highest area comes in the field of
science, including medicine. The third area is that of entertainment, although the high profile salaries of professional ath-
letes, TV and movie personalities give a certain unreality to
this salary situation. Less than 5 per cent of the nation's 40,000
actors received more than $25,000 in 1982. The next area is
that of skilled labor which may very will reflect the success of
the labor movement in forcing up these salaries. The lowest
area includes those attempting to teach, promote or enforce
personal or community values, excepting lawyers who seem to
be in a class by themselves.

The Value Imbalance

Money, science, entertainment, skilled labor, and lastly
personal and social values seem to be the American salary
hierarchy. Some economists insist that in a market economy

wages reflect the value we place on the product. If that is true, then money is first, values last. One can see in this an ethical climate conducive to the firestorm of greed which we are describing. The money fixation is draining away our best people from these more value-oriented professions. *Newsweek* (May 26, '86) commented on research showing that the "brightest and the best" of our recent graduates are seeking their fortunes on Wall Street. More than 25 per cent of the 1986 graduating class from the Harvard Business School took jobs at investment banking firms. That report states that over 400 resumes were received by First Boston from graduating seniors at Yale University alone.

The MacNeil-Lehrer report (9/9/87) recently charged that the fixation on making money is also killing the teaching profession. One example would be Wilberforce University, a predominantly black college in Ohio, having no teachers in its recent graduating class. Most went into law, medicine and other higher paying professions. It is estimated that unless there is a change in values by the year 2000, the percentage of black teachers, which is now 15 per cent, will have dropped to 5 per cent. We can deplore the scarcity of good teachers and the quality of our education, but the hard fact is that we get what we are willing to pay for.

The harder question is whether or not this salary situation really represents the values which Americans want to hold. Do we really put the abundance of cash first in our value system, then consumer goods and productivity, then science and health, then entertainment, and finally, at the very bottom, education, justice, ethics and religion? Or does this signify something more subtle, more sinister, within the social body which is more an illness warping our judgments than a consciously chosen set of values?

The Demise of the Protestant Work Ethic

The problem is often described in terms of the loss of the

so-called "Protestant work ethic." This is a term usually attributed to the philosopher Max Weber in his book, *The Protestant Ethic and the Spirit of Capitalism*. Arising after the Reformation in the sixteenth century, capitalism is a relatively new phenomenon. Max Weber characterized it as the social counterpart to the theology of John Calvin. The previous attitude had been that unlimited desire for gain was both anti-social and immoral. Capitalism therefore represented a radical change in moral standards where that which had been a vice now became a virtue. Initially, this new attitude was part of a religious reformation stressing both the sovereignty of God and the freedom of men and women to control their own destinies, but always under that primary allegiance to God. Weber describes it as the glorification of work as a divine calling, the freedom to labor without being forced, the making of money as an end in itself, hard work as a moral duty, and what he called the "spirit of Christian asceticism," which prevented this from becoming an exercise in hedonism.

The problem was, as Weber described it, that capitalism began as the practical idealism of the aspiring bourgeoisie, but ended as "an orgy of materialism." Later capitalism departed from this original Godly discipline and control of the economic enterprise and became a more individualistic resistance to any interference in matters of business from either the church or the state.

Weber called this "the Spirit of Calvinism." But R.H. Tawney, in his introduction to Weber's book, calls this second individualistic phase a perversion of Calvinism. It was part of the general intellectual movement coming out of the Reformation, reflected in both Protestant and Catholic writers. This represented in the seventeenth and eighteenth centuries primarily a loss of capitalism's religious rootage in a sovereign God. It was replaced by the Utilitarian movement, as expressed by Jeremy Bentham, John Stuart Mill and others, and the escalation of individualism until as Weber put it, "the spirit of religious asceticism . . . has escaped from the cage." It is to this perversion of Calvinism that we should look for the historical source of the Greed Syndrome coming to such peculiar force today. When Calvinism was replaced by Utilitarianism, then capitalism turned to an orgy of materialism. The central cause was the loss of Calvin's sovereign God, whose justice puts restraints on the overweening greed of the human animal.

Paul Bernstein, in an article in *The Wharton Magazine* (Vol. 4, #33, '80, 194) points to recent studies showing that today the American labor force has largely accepted a new attitude toward work, "that is secular and self-centered." This new work ethic is part of the individual desire for meaningful and challenging labor directed to self-fulfillment and is unrelated to religious demands or to the welfare of the community. As Daniel Yankelovich put it in *Work in America: The Decade Ahead*, ('79, xx) "Americans want to fulfill the dream of a full and rich life and see the building of an ethic . . . around obligations to self rather than obligations to others." Our study would suggest that the primary symbol of meaning and self-fulfillment in this new work ethic is that of money.

The Invisible Hand and the Ghost of Adam Smith

When capitalism lost its Calvinist commitment to the sovereign God, it was quickly replaced by another, supplied in the 18th century by Adam Smith. (*Wealth of Nations*) This was the economic law of supply and demand. Smith called it the doctrine of the "Invisible Hand." Leave it alone (laissez faire), because greed is the only proper dynamic for running an economy and self-interest will eventually rectify any problems, according to the immutable laws, the "Invisible Hand," of supply and demand. To this was then added the Social Darwinism which applied the discoveries of the new biology to many other aspects of society. Darwin's laws of the survival of the fittest were found in the 19th century to be congenial to Smith's earlier economic analysis. With the aid of men like Spencer, these immutable laws of nature were progressively deified and applied to society in general and economics in particular.

The laissez-faire economics of Adam Smith dominated the early life of America. But with the coming of the great depression, faith in this approach was sorely shaken. The Roosevelt New Deal represented the full scale turning from "leave it alone" economics to a more-and-more tightly planned economy. In the years that followed, with the work of men like John Kenneth Galbraith, this type of government-controlled economics became normative and also was identified with the Democratic party.

In more recent years, with the emergence of more and more moderate Democratic economic policies and with the resurgence of the Republican party, the "demand side" economics of the New Deal has been replaced with the so-called "supply side" policies of the Reagan administration where governmental control of the economy has been systematically loosened. Along with this has gone a vigorous resurrection of Adam Smith and his laissez-faire economics and the escalation of the Greed Syndrome. The combination of the loss of God in modern society, the shift toward self-fulfillment in the work ethic and the return of laissez-faire economics is clearly the climate that has fueled the upsurge of greed in this decade.

Functional Atheism

The wellspring of this return to economic Darwinism is the loss of belief in a sovereign God. As Weber insisted, it was when Calvinism was replaced by the absent watchmaker God of Deism and then atheistic Utilitarianism that capitalism turned to an orgy of materialism. Bentham's philosophy, that whatever is useful is right, has a close similarity to John Dewey's dominant American Pragmatism that bases what is right upon that which works. And these are essentially God-rejecting or at best God-avoiding philosophies. What happens with these approaches to life is that if there is no sovereign God upon whom we can base our understanding of right and wrong, then we either make a God out of the process of history or nature or economics, or we deify human beings and set ourselves up as the final arbiters of what works. Modern laissez-faire economics is intrinsically atheistic for in it we have deified the process. The laws of economics are in charge of the universe. Since we can do nothing about them, we must leave them alone and, incidentally, exploit them to our own advantage.

This raises a host of problems. The one we have been concentrating on here is the dramatic escalation of greed which has accompanied the return of Adam Smith. Another is the great imbalance between the very wealthy and the very poor. A third is the creation of a value system that puts money at the top and then everything else before a concern for abiding values. This provides an ethical vacuum which is an ideal breeding ground for unbridled self-interest, the neglect of the poor and the twisting of the machinery of justice to our own selfish ends.

Leave it alone. Let the poor starve for that is nature's way of righting the imbalance. Let it alone, for the invisible hand of supply and demand will eventually correct the salary scale however many get ground up in the meantime. Let it alone. Business has no interest in ethics for that means tinkering with the economic system. One looks in vain for courses on ethics in the many business schools of our nation. And if there is no God, and if the system, or the most aggressive human beings are all we have to go on, then this is right. What else is there? And, consequently, we might as well give up hope and enjoy ourselves by getting as much of the pie as we can before going out in a blaze of nuclear glory. This kind of functional atheism is the dead center of the Greed Syndrome.

An Ethically Conscious Alternative

But the Hebrew-Christian ethic has always offered hope instead of despair. This is centered upon the premise that there is a God who transcends all races and cultures, all systems and natural forces. And from this basic premise, certain positive and hopeful things inevitably follow. It begins by challenging the primary assumptions of modern laissez-faire economics which is a form of what is called "reductionism," in this case reducing everything to economics. Yes, we live in a world governed by economic law; but we also live in a world governed by physical laws and psychological laws and social and ethical laws, all of which affect our lives. And these are all modified by one of the profoundest laws of all. As human beings, we are free and responsible creatures, capable of altering our environment, of changing things for the better or the worse. And behind and beyond it all is the fundamental fact of the universe: God is the sovereign lord of creation. He is a God of justice who places us all under his judgment and commands us to use the various laws of these universal processes as good stewards in his service. There is only one force in the universe capable of controlling, directing and chastening the inordinate and insatiable self-interest of the human animal and that is a sovereign God. Therein lies our hope.

Now let's see how that works in terms of the salary situation we have been discussing. A concern for value in economics demands self-conscious ethical judgments and points in the direction of an ethically planned economy. With regard to this immediate topic, it would seem that at times the Invisible Hand of supply and demand does not automatically work for the good of all persons or the quality of society. It is a ponderous, callous, impersonal process, indifferent to human need and social and religious values, sorely needing to be humanized and ethicized. What it has done in recent years is allow the salary situation to be dominated by the drive to make more and more money, irrespective of the values it supports or the disparity it creates between the very, very rich and the very, very poor. The "spirit of religious asceticism," which Weber said had escaped from the cage, needs to be recaptured if capitalism is to survive. That is the needed restraint, the ethical brakes, on the magnificent, mighty, efficient machine called capitalism.

The Hebrew Christian Ethic of Work and Salary

What we are looking for is an ethic of work and salary that is adequate for the task of saving our economic system from what some are predicting is certain disaster. The first thing that has to be done is dethrone Mammon and replace it with the sovereign God of Justice. We need to rediscover the value system that generated capitalism in the first place. Jesus summarized the ethical tradition of Moses and the prophets in a brilliant one-liner: "Seek first the kingdom (sovereignty) of God and his righteousness (justice), and all these things shall be yours as well." (Matt. 6:32) Amos made this point for the prophetic Old Testament: "What does the Lord require of you but to do justice, love mercy and walk humbly with your God?" (Micah 6:8) Mammon is only dethroned by enthroning the true Lord of the universe.

The implications of putting God first are that, for the kingdom ethic, the things of the Spirit are more important than the things of the flesh. This is behind what Weber called the spirit of Christian asceticism, where living simply and avoiding extravagance are a natural extension of this priority. Furthermore, principle is more important than profit. Quality, service, integrity come before our concern for salary. God's eternal plan is more important than temporal advantage. The Kingdom of God concentrates on the quality of human life rather than its quantity.

Already we are in trouble. Whether or not we personally accept that value priority, the telltale signs of our salary scale tell us that the things of the material world would seem clearly to be more important than those of the world of values. We concentrate on the quantity of cash instead of the quality of our work or its meaning for our lives. Mammon has simply reversed the priorities of the ethic that began the capitalist revolution. No wonder so many are noticing a basic change in our modern economic philosophy.

The next basic theological fact about the Hebrew-Christian ethic is that this sovereign God is a God of Justice, or righteousness, for the two words are synonymous. This is the overwhelmingly dominant description of the nature of God in both Old and New Testaments. Living according to this ethic then becomes a matter of reflecting in our lives the justice of God. Within this framework, the question is how much salary is justified in the light of the Hebrew-Christian ethic? When does a justified self-interest become unjustified? What is a just wage? In other words, where does the greed-line begin?

Justice and the Ethic of Work

This is essentially a theological question for it becomes a matter of understanding the nature of God and his justice. In both Old and New Testaments, the justice of God is described as a balance between four great concepts: God's love and his wrath, his command and the freedom he gives us to obey or disobey. All of these together describe the justice of God. In sharpening this ponderous concept so that we can apply it to the deceptively simple matter of determining what is a just wage, there are certain ethical strategies that can be derived from these four concepts.

(1) The love of God in the Bible describes his redeeming presence in our lives. This love overflows with goodwill and is concerned for the dignity and fulfillment of persons. It represents God's intention to provide appropriate rewards for righteousness, for faithfulness, for good work. (Mark 10:30) God's love reaches out to individuals in order to help them grow and achieve a good life, with dignity and honor, with work that encourages us to be our best selves. God's love is a relationship that points us toward the development of loving relationships with all men and women. When salaries or wages reflect and augment this set of concerns, then they can be said at that point to be justified. When they don't, they stand under the judgment of God.

(2) The wrath of God in the Bible describes his willingness to allow us to reject his love and to experience the harsh

realities of that rejection. Wrath is the divine mystery that permits sin, suffering and death in the world. This, too, is part of God's justice. Translated into economic strategy, this suggests that income can destroy us whether it be too little or too much. The disparity of income, if too great, can spoil relationships and create social strife. Wages that are too high or too low can hinder our relationship with God as Jesus pointed out in his discussion with the rich young ruler. (Matt. 19:16-22) The wrath of God demands that men and women must be punished when their desire for wealth prompts them to seek more than is just for themselves and so violate the law of love for others. The wrath of God allows for differences in ability, motivation, training and achievement, and so, inevitably, for differences in salary. This is the mystery of evil and only makes theological sense when seen as just one element in the totality of God's justice. God's wrath is inextricably entwined with his love. It is his love in agony, accepting the cause and effect necessities of his own creation, but redeeming those harsh realities with the availability of his presence. Wrath is only unjust when divorced from the redemptive activity of God's love. This, God never does; but he allows us to do it and this is its own punishment.

(3) The command of God is the inevitable product of his sovereignty. It is God being himself. It is the Creator's declaration that we live in a universe of order and structure which abides by certain laws among which are those of economics and morality. His basic ethical law is that we must reflect his justice in our lives for that is the way the universe works whether we like it or not. This means that the rule of law must be established and maintained if we are to live in a just society. Without this, civilization disintegrates for that is the way our existence has been structured by a sovereign and just Creator. One can see here how the rule of law and the fabric of society are threatened by the prevailing functional atheism of our day. As the young priest in Dostoevsky's novel *Brothers Karamazov* said to his atheist student brother Ivan, "If there is no God, then everything is permissible," in this case, even the murder

of his father.

When sharpened to the point of economics and the salary question, this says that the rewards of society should be in keeping with the nature of a just God. Money is a means to God's end not an end in itself. Work is a divine calling that should give meaning to life. Whatever happens in the marketplace stands under the judgment of God in the light of his purity and faithfulness, his love and integrity. God's love is a command and we are indeed responsible for our brothers and sisters, as the Apostle Paul insisted: "If your brother is being injured by what you eat, you are no longer walking in love." (Ro. 14:15)

The wrath of God is also a command. This means that the drive for self-gratification, so necessary for our survival and the health of our economy, must also be restrained. A just wage is therefore a restrained wage under the constraints of God's love and the threats of his punishment. And we see here that the laissez-faire commitment to the impersonal laws of supply and demand violates God's justice. For there are other laws of a commanding God. The unrestrained accumulation of wealth would seem to be contrary to the justice of God and so to stand under his judgment. This entire book is a description of what this drive for more is doing to our nation.

(4) Finally, the justice of God is also the charter of our freedom. Since freedom is an expression of the justice of God, it is also one of the most basic needs of the human personality. There must be a freedom to sin if one wills and to make essential choices that may go against our best interest if that is our determination. For we are human beings and not animals and, therefore, responsible for our judgments. So we must be free to do good or to do evil; nothing in society or in our own lives must deprive us of that freedom. But this freedom is part of God's justice. It must be in balance with his law and his love and chastened by his wrath.

When brought to focus on the question of a just salary, this translates into a wage that liberates us from the constraints that would deny that freedom. Poverty is a denial of freedom for life and dignity and the enjoyment of the fruits of the earth; thus it violates the justice of God. Excessive wealth, on the other hand, not only hinders the freedom of others, but it can become a form of slavery to the wealthy, condemning them, as Jesus put it, to a quantitative anxiety over things, consuming their time and energies and stultifying an appreciation of the qualitative things of the spirit. Ultimately, greed drives men and women from each other and from God. The worship of Mammon is, after all, really the worship of ourselves. But God is not mocked for the penalties of his wrath are built into the very process itself. Where does a just salary become an exercise in greed? When it begins to violate the justice of God.

This will vary with the individual and the circumstances. The salary strategies operating in our economy reflect this. The normal guidelines, in effect more by default than design, insist that salaries should be based on whatever the market will bear or on the law of supply and demand. These impersonal standards, however, apply more rightly to the price of goods and tend to do violence to persons. If they could be disciplined by the justice of God, then it would be possible for them to be fair and effective salary norms; but this is not generally the case. Other criteria, like hard work, ability, education and training are determiners of salary which can be more justly applied. The one norm most compatible with the Biblical concept of justice is that salaries are an expression of the importance of the job, the faithfulness of the employee and the genuine value created for society.

The salary priorities of our study suggest, however, that, instead of these kinds of concerns, George Bernard Shaw's cynical comment better describes our situation: "The price of ability does not depend on merit but on supply and demand." If the salary situation is any indication, we do not seem to be a value-oriented society. Our values are those of the god Mammon rather than the God of the Bible. If this is what we want, then we should make this choice consciously and be prepared for the consequences. If not, then it is time we re-examine our salary priorities in terms of some defensible ethical standards.

Chapter 4

I Want Something For Nothing

"Sin is in as a moneymaker." This is the catch line in a recent report by *The Wall Street Journal* (Feb. 7, '86, 42) on how the states are increasingly turning to the lottery as what someone has called "the alchemist's stone of painless taxation." A major social change is taking place as gambling in America, for the first time in our history, is being formally legitimatized, not only by law, but primarily by what Vicki Abt, James Smith and Eugene Christiansen, in their book *The Business of Risk*, identify as social institutions within a changing cultural context. Commercial gambling is entering the American social structure and assuming a place alongside sports, theme amusement parks, television and packaged vacations as a major leisure-activity institution. They point to a tug of war taking place between the fading authority of moral and religious anti-gambling sentiment and the burgeoning power of institutionalized commercial gambling.

"Have you caught the fever?" This common gimmick for TV lottery promotion well describes the current scene. Everyone has gotten into the act from celebrities offering fabulous fortunes within the magazine publishing world to TV shows of every kind with prizes and money games pandering to what they consider to be the public appetite to state governments striving to balance their insatiable budgets. One symbol for modern America is that great roulette wheel of fortune whose ratings blanket almost everything else on television. As a nation, we seem at least superficially committed to getting something for nothing.

Gambling is as old as the human condition, and its supporters insist it is a particularly American pastime. It is often pointed out that the early American government conducted lotteries to finance its venture in liberty. Harvard, Yale, Princeton and others were at least partially financed by this method. In 1807, the State of Ohio used a lottery to finance the improvement of the Cuyahoga and Muskingum rivers. Since then, the increasing financial stress placed on state governments, heightened by the various depressions in our history, has steadily, if haltingly, fed this so-called basic American urge.

The ongoing attraction of institutional gambling produced inevitable reactions within the conservative religious climate of this country. In 1835, Ohio abolished lotteries due to misleading promises and the competition from too many lotteries. By 1890 the lottery was illegal in most states, and so it remained until the 1960s when it began a comeback that has catapulted it into a prime place on the American scene.

A landmark was passed in 1970 when New York City created the Off-Track Betting Corporation. It took 18 years to accomplish this, and seems to have been a product of the chronic revenue needs of the city along with a politically expedient reaction to public demand and pressure lobbies. According to Abt, it was done without a referendum through hasty legislation that paid little attention to the needs of the racing industry or to the many social and moral objections emerging from the eighteen years of public debate.

Also symptomatic of this major social change is the experience of Ohio which passed a lottery bill in 1973 by a two to one margin. By 1974 it was completely self-sufficient, one of two revenue-raising institutions. The other is the State Liquor Board. The lottery was an instant success with 35 cents on each dollar returned to the State. By 1985 Ohio was receiving $350 million a year from the lottery with all money going to the state program in education.

For the nation, the decisive step was taken in 1984, with the approval of state lotteries in California, Oregon, Missouri and West Virginia. This extended the state lottery system to 22 states and effectively completed the evolution of state lotteries from a dubious and initially unsuccessful experiment in public finance to a normal function of the state government. The pressure now on the non-lottery states is intense. Few are expected to hold out. Parimutuel betting has also increased dramatically. Not so with gambling casinos, due to the many legal, social and ethical problems said to surround them.

But What of the Ethical Question?

It would seem that Abt is correct that the lotterization of America is essentially accomplished. It is also becoming more and more apparent that the ethical and social consequences are unresolved. We are just now in the midst of a massive shift in ethical values of which this upsurge in gambling and lottery fever is merely one of many symptoms. The initial descriptive study done by the Commission on the Review of the National Policy Toward Gambling, so well analyzed by Abt, Smith and Christiansen, has made quite clear that these phenomena raise profound ethical questions which we as a nation are not generally skilled in answering. So the need is to go beyond the mere observing and cataloguing of a fascinating phenomenon to the deeper analysis of the ethical questions which strike at the very root of our national strength.

Money is the Heart of It

One of the most attractive features of the lottery package is the lure of state revenue gathered without pain from a multitude eager to donate to this cause. The burgeoning demands on state budgets are well known and lotteries promise to be the most efficient way of easing the strain. The players have fun, the state wins, and our taxes do not increase. What could be more attractive?

Yet there are several tactical problems with this rosy picture. In the first place, according to a study conducted by the Tax Foundation Inc., lotteries are actually very inefficient ways to raise money. As reported by sociology professor David Guldin, state governments normally pay about one and a half to two per cent to collect tax moneys. The cost to collect money through state lotteries is between 26 and 60 per cent. It is true that in Ohio 35 per cent of all lottery money goes to state education; but this amounts to only 6 to 8 per cent of the total budget. It has been estimated that a one quarter of one per cent increase in the Ohio State Income tax would equal all that the lottery contributes to the state treasury.

The claim to efficiency in the short run is often countered with a warning that in the long run risky chance and sudden wealth unconnected with the production of goods and services violate the principles of disciplined monetary efficiency which economist and social philosopher Max Weber called the sound basis of social institutions. (Abt p. 154) It is true that since its institution, California's lottery has been able to raise about $200 million a month. But according to a report on NBC News (6/10/86), under this lottery financing California has gone from one of the best to one of the worst education systems in the nation. The cause and effect relationship is, of course, a matter of debate. At least, it would seem clear that the lottery has not been a panacea. One of the tactical problems is that lotteries tend to make it more difficult for states to enact normal tax legislation. A recent ad on Cleveland TV Channel 5 (10/14/88) urged people not to allow the 6 per cent lottery subsidy to dull their concern to vote taxes to finance the schools. There is some suggestion that the rosy picture of lottery-financed state programs is a flash in the pan, seemingly effective for the short run, but in the long run so filled with problems that it may be a Trojan horse.

The deeper problem lies with another aspect of the Greed Syndrome. Voluntary taxes raised by lotteries seem on the surface to work so well that politicians soon want more and more. Fueled by the insatiable public demand for additional social services, but without the taxes which any socialist government knows are necessary to sustain such programs, there comes into operation what Abt calls the "Revenue Imperative." Unrestrained government will continue to demand more and more revenue from gambling and this will destroy any possible benefits. The state governments get more and more aggressively into the business of organized gambling with intensified advertising campaigns and the passing of gambling laws which result in an increase in government claims on wagering. This raises the cost to the player who has a minuscule chance at a decreasing percentage of the lottery dollar. As Abt suggests, this transforms gambling into a social institution that serves government purposes rather than individual needs. Governments can be greedy as well as individuals.

The pattern is the same. The revenue imperative operating within state legislatures is just another way of describing the Greed Syndrome and these are some of its symptoms. Under the laudable guise of serving the public good, the state allows itself to be caught up in the oldest game in town: making a fast buck the quickest and easiest way, but with a series of consequences which are, to say the least, debatable. It is instructive to note that the government Commission on Gambling concludes with many warnings concerning the state's raising of revenue through lotteries which can "warp the budgetary process" and "sacrifice the best interests of the public to the desire to obtain revenue." Without apparently intending to be, this report is actually a warning against the institutionalization of the Greed Syndrome.

Does It Reduce Illegal Gambling?

Another tactical matter has to do with the effect of state-controlled gambling on reducing illegal gambling. The first concern is whether or not one is more attractive than the other. According to Abt, while the government takes about 6 cents from every dollar bet at racetracks and frontons and about 7.5 cents of every dollar lost at casinos, it keeps from 40 to 45 cents of every dollar used to buy lottery tickets. Sociologist Guldin points out that the average casino in Las Vegas gives a 95 per cent return on money wagered. For slot machines, the house retains 5 to 25 per cent. If you play jai alai in Florida, the house earnings are 13-15 per cent. The average bookmaker keeps only 5 per cent. With state lotteries, it is a dramatically different picture making the other forms of gambling far more attractive. Looking at the 22 states with lottery systems, the state keeps an average of 55 per cent on weekly games, 49 per cent on daily games and 55 per cent on instant games. The odds are obviously in favor of non-lottery legalized gambling. It has been estimated that the odds against picking the right 6 out of 48 numbers in the New York State lottery are one in 12.3 million. No commercial casino would survive with those odds. Illegal bookies give much better odds and, according to Guldin, there are other advantages like credit or same day payoffs that give illegal gambling a competitive edge.

Empirically, there seems to be no indication from recent studies that lotteries cut down illegal gambling. Gulden points out that in several states studied closely, illegal gambling increased with the introduction of State lotteries. New York is a good example. Two surveys were done, one by the Associated Press, and one by the New York City police department. Both studies, after interviewing bookies, gamblers and others involved, concluded that the State lotteries were not drawing people away from illegal gambling. They were, in effect, developing new converts. The existence of the State lotteries stimulated business. For example, after New York legalized off-track betting, it was estimated that bets made to illegal bookies increased by 25 per cent.

How Does Gambling Work? Ethical Strategy

When does gambling become an ethical problem that is more than a mere tactical matter of efficiency or expediency? When does it become pathological in ways that strike deeply at the heart of personal or national health? These are questions of strategies, or ethical principles, and in the long run are more serious than the usual concern over tactics. Within the framework of the Judeo-Christian ethic, the answer to this question has to begin with theology. When gambling, like any other intensely pleasurable activity, violates the sovereignty and justice of God, then it has become pathological and comes under God's judgment. At this point, a normal self-interest has turned to greed, and we can talk about symptoms of the Greed Syndrome.

This is a very heavy answer. But within this religious tradition there are many aids to sharpen such an abstract answer into the kinds of strategies that can be grasped and applied to specific problems. Jesus gave his disciples one clue in his summary of the law and the prophets: "Love the Lord your God with all your heart and soul and mind and strength, and your neighbor as yourself." (Mark 12:28-34) In this brilliant summary of the Old Testament that anyone in his audiences could accept, Jesus points to the three directions to which we must look in deciding how well a particular action corresponds to the sovereignty and justice of God: the upward look to God, the inward look to self, and the outward look to other people.

Does Gambling Involve Our Relation to God?

Loving God totally means that God comes first as the guiding force and norm of one's life. This puts God ahead of self-interest. Here is the crux of the entire matter. What are our priorities? Jesus' answer was unequivocal: "Seek first the kingdom of God..." This is the initial step in what is called Christian (or Hebrew) stewardship. When God is central in a man or woman's life, there are many things they can do without harm to themselves, if they do them according to the divine will. One of them may very well be to gamble. But without some commitment to a power beyond themselves, the danger is increased of being unable to stem the downward plunge of human *eros* with its many destructive symptoms of greed and self-interest. With something that can be as pleasurable as gambling, one needs to pay special attention to this danger.

The Bible describes God's nature as that of justice, or righteousness. According to this upward look, it is the total balance between reward and punishment, law and freedom, which constitutes God's justice and defines what the Judeo-Christian ethic means by what works. It is not enough to say that something like a state lottery works, for greed works very well if we define it in terms of immediate gratification with a minimal regard for the consequences.

More exactly, God's love is permissive and demands that men and women be able to experience the good things of life. This might well include the benefits of gambling. But we must not stop here, for the rewards of God's love are part of his justice. There are requirements surrounding the gifts of life. It is here that the philosophy of getting something for nothing runs into the most trouble with the Hebrew-Christian ethic. It has lifted reward out of context with no concern for the commands and conditions of God's justice. Winnings from gambling are not a reward for righteousness, or faithfulness, or intelligence, or hard work or devotion to anything except one's own self-interest. Gambling creates no value; it merely moves money around under a unique form of illusion, what someone has called a cynical deception of value not received. On these terms, gambling cannot be called a just use of money.

Or take the imperative of God's justice. When applied to any human activity, it requires that if justice is to be preserved, the rule of law must be established within every area of life and, having been established, must be enforced. The legalization of gambling raises this question in a new way. Do lotteries promote or hinder the rule of law within the states? We have already noted that instead of restraining illegal gambling, lotteries have, in fact, in New York State contributed to its increase. Abt reminds us that in the nineteenth century state-franchised and regulated private lotteries ended in scandals and disaster. No doubt one could argue that such need not be the case again. It is to their credit that state lottery boards are determined to be scrupulous in their enforcement of the law. One symptom of the destructive presence of the Greed Syndrome is whether a particular activity tends to promote dishonesty and destroy integrity. We have said that greed represents a normal and healthy self-interest turned pathological. There are already questions being raised about the cynical distortion of lottery advertising. State lotteries are required by law to make clear to the public the probabilities of winning. They do so, not on the tickets, but in booklets in microscopic print available at sales outlets. It is the amount of the prize, not the probability of winning that is the basis of lottery advertising. Misleading advertising is a form of dishonesty that signals a very subtle disintegration of integrity and a very real attack upon the rule of law. Violation of statute law can be easily detected. The committing of false witness is more subtle, more dangerous, and harder to detect and enforce. Whether or not state-controlled gambling encourages the disintegration of ethical integrity is the deeper and ultimately more important matter. One is not guilty by association, but operating in a highly contagious environment like that of gambling always puts one at greater risk.

The question is often raised about whether gambling is an appropriate function of state government. This involves the distinction between what is legal and what is fitting according to some ethical standard. The Apostle Paul was much concerned about the ethical application of the teachings of Jesus to his own times. In his letter to the Corinthians, he makes a strong point. "All things are lawful for me, but not all things are helpful." (I Cor. 5:12) Civil law is not the primary concern for children of God; much that is lawful is not necessarily ethical. Our greater concern should be over what is morally fitting within the Judeo-Christian context which, for Paul, was the divine purpose for any particular function: "the body is not *meant* (by God) for immorality." (*porneia*; I Cor. 6:13)

Paul used the word *porneia* to refer to the prostitution of the sex function. The principle also applies to other intensely pleasurable activities when they become ends in themselves, like money and getting something for nothing. When the economic system, which, within the Hebrew-Christian tradition, is to provide for the necessities of life, becomes a plaything and an end in itself, then we have prostituted what Martin Luther called that "order" of society. In one way or another, self-destructive forces go into operation. These are themselves symptoms of the Greed Syndrome. Paul insisted that "God will destroy both one and the other." (I Cor. 6:13) The judgment of God is built into the very fabric of life. Does gambling correspond with God's purpose for the economic order of his creation? If not, then it is highly inappropriate as a function of a state government dedicated to economic health and pretending to be under God.

Is Gambling Helpful to Persons?

Some of the most destructive results of gambling have to do with the welfare of persons. It is here that capitalism most often clashes with the Hebrew-Christian ethic. It is often pointed out that gambling in general, and lotteries in particular, can have a devastating effect on individuals. This is especially sensitive when one considers the nature of the activity and of those who play. Gambling appeals to certain intensely pleasurable sensations accompanying the getting of something for nothing: self-interest, desperation, boredom, frustrated desire for power or security or recognition. These are all very normal, human and essentially healthy, providing we handle them properly. For the emotionally, physically and socially strong, these motives can, no doubt, be kept in their proper place; but for the weak, they can be disastrous. Self-interest becomes greed when it is out of control. For the poor, gambling becomes a form of regressive taxation where the burden of the state's desire to raise money, for however noble an end, falls most heavily on those who can least afford it. It is pleasant for those who are playing. But so is freezing to death.

The question of the dangers to mental health have been addressed by Dr. Charles Custer, Chief of Mental Health, Veterans Hospital, Brecksville, Ohio. This physician and his associates started several treatment centers for psychological withdrawal from the gambling obsession. The symptoms and recovery tactics are much like those of alcohol and drug addiction. Excitement is what so many obsessive gamblers seem to crave, rather than money. Gambling is a form of delusion and withdrawal from reality. Abt comments that "these are not lofty dreams, but illusions which are counterproductive because nothing a player can do can make them come true." The result is that families are hurt and resentful, often ending in divorce and other forms of social disintegration. Today it is reported there are 582 chapters of groups patterned after Alcoholics Anonymous in 38 states for recovering gambling addicts. Complete withdrawal is the therapy: "I won't buy another lottery ticket," was the pledge of one recovering obsessive gambler. Whether or not it is morally legitimate for a state to abet an addiction is the crucial question.

The Apostle Paul, in applying the teachings of Jesus to such practical problems as what foods to eat in that kosher society, came up with another ethical strategy which seems to apply to the problem we are raising: "whatever causes my brother to stumble." (Ro. 14:21) Within the Christian ethic, we are called to "walk in love." (Eph. 5:2) This means we are our brothers' and sisters' keepers. Perhaps we ourselves are strong enough to do certain things without being hurt; but no one walks alone. We are part of a human family where everything we do affects someone else. This ethic of concern calls us to live in the light of compassionate responsibility.

Within this Christian ethic we are called to grow up into what Paul called "the fullness of the stature of Christ" (Eph.

4:13), what Micah would probably have called "walking humbly with your God." The question, then, becomes, does gambling contribute to moral, spiritual, social, economic maturity?

One of Paul's pivotal criteria for such growth is freedom: "I will not be enslaved by anything." (I Cor. 6:12) Among the most sensitive problems is the way in which people sometimes get trapped in an obsession and literally lose their freedom. At this point the "Lottery Fever" slogan comes most sharply under scrutiny. A fever is normally a symptom of an illness. It may be that through intensive advertising our freedom to resist the obsessions of gambling and the lottery craze is being rapidly curtailed. Stephen De John of the Ohio State Lottery Commission points to an 89 per cent increase in advertising budgets for lotteries in the nation during the year 1986 with $501 million going to agents in the form of commissions. In Ohio alone, there are 5500 sales agents and a steady barrage of TV commercials urging us to "catch the fever." As Abt puts it, the "business of risk is replacing naturally occurring gambling behaviors...designed to produce maximum losses from the maximum number of people." In the words of John Bergin, U.S. president of the advertising agency, McCann Erickson Worldwide, at the 1985 meeting of the North American Association of State Lotteries, "What other business offers such fantastic dreams and such little hope?" (*Wall Street Journal*, 2/7/86)

British gaming laws do not permit this kind of advertising. The Royal Commission (1978) places gambling under severe legal restraints in order to discourage what they call socially damaging excesses. The British plan which permits, but discourages, seems to be much more in keeping with the Judeo-Christian ethic of the justice of God than what is emerging as the American system of permitting and radically encouraging with a veritable advertising blitz. Again, the Greed Syndrome is operating in full force through state lottery advertising, threatening to undo whatever benefits may otherwise accrue.

What About the Protestant Work Ethic?

Daniel Bell, Harvard sociologist, lists as one of the major "cultural contradictions of capitalism" the anomaly that occurs as the radical hedonism of the contemporary mood competes with our traditional Protestant work ethic. Nowhere is this more visible than within the escalating gambling mania. One of the latest symptoms is the Big Cypress Bingo parlor erected on a Seminole Indian reservation in a Florida swamp, holding 5600 people at a time. Every Saturday and Sunday morning, players are bussed and flown in from all over the U.S., Canada, and many foreign countries. Prizes range from a few dollars to $125,000 or a beach front condominium. Steve Blad, owner and founder, claims he took in $15 million in 1987. (*Time*, April 25, '88) The contradiction in all of this is between what Daniel Bell calls the necessities of production, which demand the disciplined virtues of the Protestant ethic, and the realities of the consumer public, caught up as they seem to be in an escalating mood of hedonism. Gambling stands at the intersection of these two aspects of American life and the outcome is still in doubt.

The Christian ethic has always insisted that work is a necessary ingredient in physical rewards. As the Apostle Paul put it, "To one who works, his wages are not reckoned as a gift, but as his due." (Ro. 4:4) The most common metaphor used by Jesus to describe his disciples was that of servants working in the master's vineyard. The rewards for faithful service were not all spiritual rewards for he was realistic about the physical rewards of "lands and houses and treasure on earth" that accrue from dedication to the justice of God. (Mark 10:30) For him, and for Christians ever since, the truth has been that physical prosperity, although not inevitable nor necessarily deserved as Job assumed, is generally one of the benefits of the honesty, integrity and devotion to duty incumbent upon the servants of a just God.

But Jesus went even more deeply into the human condition in his parable of the laborers in the vineyard. (Matt. 20:1-

16) There we see that it is the unemployed laborers them-selves, rather than the demands of the vineyard, who desper-ately need this work: "Why do you stand here idle all day?" The concept of reward has much more meaning here in terms of our need for God's sovereign presence in our lives. But one aspect of this message seems to be that meaningful labor itself is an important necessity for mental, spiritual and social health. Ask anyone who has been out of work for any length of time.

Now it is this fact of Western Christian culture that most social historians point to as the foundation of the capitalistic system, a willingness, even a desire, to work hard for the avail-able rewards. And it is just here that the termites seem to be nibbling at the woodwork. The escalating mood of getting something for nothing is one expression of the Greed Syn-drome that is focused dramatically in the gambling phenom-enon. Whether the capitalistic economy can survive this attack is the kind of question being asked today, not only by ethicists, but most forcefully by sociologists like Daniel Bell.

The ethical strategies we have been discussing come to focus in the question, when does gambling become pathologi-cal? Or, one could ask, when does a natural interest in risk become part of the Greed Syndrome? The answers to which we have been led point in a consistent direction: when gam-bling contravenes the law; when it gets out of control; when it comes first in one's list of moral priorities; when it injures persons; when it hinders personal or social growth to maturity; when it becomes an end in itself. That is, when it takes over a person's life. These are all symptoms of the Greed Syndrome in operation within the institution of gambling.

Chapter 5

We Must Make a Profit

It all depends on one's definition of success. We really must make a profit if the capitalist economy is to survive. But in an ethical context we cannot define success purely in terms of profit for, from this standpoint, the rewards of life are the by-product of a deeper commitment to ethical values that are in tune with the structure of the universe. This faces us with the problem confronted by all nations through the centuries founded on the Hebrew-Christian ethic: how can we make a return on our investment, which seems to require a dedicated commitment to profit, while at the same time operating according to an ethic which demands a rigorous restraint on self-interest? Are these concerns incompatible? This is the ethical heart of the American capitalist dilemma.

Threats to American Industry

Corporate America is under attack. The traditional bastion of our economic strength is facing one of the most difficult periods in its post-war history. This comes principally in the form of a series of threats both within and outside of industry and the stakes are survival itself. The ethical dilemma resides both within the threats themselves and in industry responses to them. This is a corporate problem in the largest sense, involving not only jobs, stockholders and factories, but corporations, entire industries and the American economy in general.

One of the most serious threats comes from international competition. We have had it all our own way since World War II when America emerged as the strongest nation on earth. We literally swamped Japan and Germany with the output of our economy. In 1960, the United States had 25 per cent of the world market share in manufacturing. Within the U.S. market, American companies produced 95 per cent of the autos, steel and consumer electronics sold. But as we rebuilt other nations, they began to compete with us. By 1979, the U.S. share in world manufacturing slipped to just over 17 per cent. Its share of its own domestic market dropped to 79 per cent for autos, 86 per cent for steel, and less than 50 per cent for consumer electronics. From 1973 to 1981, productivity growth changed from an annual 3 per cent increase to a decrease of about 0.4 per cent. So we are beleaguered by the very world we reconstructed. And we don't quite know how to handle it. The economic machine that won the war and rebuilt a world is now middle-aged, often out of date, and showing signs of wear.

Stanley Gault, CEO of Rubbermaid Corp. and president of the National Association of Manufacturers, sees overseas competition as one of the most serious threats to American industry. The U.S. balance of trade deficit is running at a record high of almost $170 billion per year, much of it in capital goods and high-tech products that were once the mainstay of our trade performance. Smart, aggressive competitors are chipping away at our markets, some from places whose names we can't even pronounce. John Naisbitt describes as a current megatrend the fact that Japan has seized from us the position of the world's leading industrial power. In the wings are Singapore, South Korea and Brazil. As Gault puts it, "whether we like it or not, this country is involved in a competitive battle across oceans and national borders for the sales and orders that are available." This is producing some severe social and ethical as well as economic strains within American industry.

Two further threats come from the courts and from Wall Street. One is the explosion of product-liability suits against industry. According to Gault, it is practically impossible to manufacture, distribute or sell a product today that won't end up in court. This has become one of the priority concerns of the NAM. The other is the consistent attack upon industry from corporate raiders. The Special Report in *Business Week* (Nov. 1986) listed Owens-Corning, Southern Union Co., Union Carbide, Goodyear and USX as current targets. The list has grown exponentially since then with Sears, Nabisco and Revlon coming under attack. A recent study aired on CBS (11/7/88) documented the continued escalation of merger mania in what looks like a feeding frenzy of sharks. T. Boone Pickens and other corporate raiders insist this is good for industries, making them in a current phrase "more lean and mean." For others, mostly within the industries and communities that support them, it has been unmitigated disaster. The essence of the CBS report was that the experience of the last year has shown that this may be good for Wall Street, but not for Main Street.

Corporate Responses and the Ethical Issues They Raise

It is no wonder, then, that corporate America is striving desperately to keep its balance and forward momentum in these difficult days. These threats have produced a host of defensive responses most of which are short-range and aimed simply at survival. The problem is that the crisis mentality within the business sector runs a serious risk of destroying the ethical base that has sustained our economy and made it great. We might win the immediate battle but end up losing the war.

Greater Efficiency Through Downsizing and Automation

One obvious response of industry has been to meet head-on the claims of inefficiency made by corporate raiders to justify their takeover attempts. There would seem little doubt that some industries have become top heavy, antiquated and mismanaged. Gault reports one medium-sized, medium-technology company that successfully responded to its foreign competition which was selling the same products for 35 to 40 per cent less. They fought back by drastically reducing their inventories and improving cash management, eliminating whole layers of management personnel, making new investments, shifting some corporate assets to product lines less vulnerable to foreign competition, and making a strong effort to crack down on 14 companies in Taiwan and Korea that were counterfeiting their products.

Citibank advertised in *Fortune* magazine and *The Wall Street Journal* that it had cut 40 per cent of its clerical force, mostly women, by installing data processing equipment. The introduction of robots into auto manufacturing, in an effort to compete with the Japanese model, is well known. A return to an emphasis on quality products is another response to the charges of inefficiency. Downsizing is a further tactic. Large corporate structures are being forced to divest themselves of subsidiary companies. There is a growing feeling within industry that it is more conducive to survival to do one thing well than many things poorly. All of this may put American industry in a more competitive situation and many of these changes are probably overdue. But such techniques also raise some important ethical questions.

For one thing, they are mostly short-term measures with little concern for the long range effect either upon themselves, the communities in which they reside, or the national economy in general. Survival is the name of the game. A sufficient cash balance to protect against take-over seems to be the major objective. The issue here is whether or not these short-term tactics where we concentrate on our own survival are mortgaging our future and doing violence to those who come after us. Living only for the present is an ethical question whether for individuals or corporations.

The practice of automation is an old problem, but is coming into prominence today as we try to fend off the Japanese. What we must realize, however, is that the Japanese operate generally according to a different ethic. Individual human life has never had the importance in the Shinto or Buddhist religions that it has within the Hebrew and Christian cultures. Jesus insisted upon the infinite worth of persons whom God loves as he marks the fall of each sparrow. Does the automation of an industry that puts men and women out of work in the name of efficiency violate this ethical strategy?

Obviously this is a disputed matter and ethically sensitive persons will differ in their answers. In terms of the Hebrew-Christian ethic, if any of these approaches to efficiency do indeed violate the justice of God, if short-range solutions take precedence over long range, if profit is more important than persons, if narrowly defined personal concerns are more important than the general welfare, then in the long run these tactics will not work. Industry and the nation will eventually be worse off than we are now. This universe and this economy only work God's way. By now, it should be abundantly clear that we are defining what works in terms of the Hebrew-Christian ethic as that which is true to the justice of God. How strange this sounds in the light of modern economic practice.

Restructuring and The Merger Mania

Another response has been what *Business Week*'s Special Report (Nov. 24, '86, 75f.) calls restructuring: "a frenzied blur of buybacks and spinoffs, mergers and acquisitions, LBO's (leverage buyouts) and recapitalizations." The purpose is to discover undervalued assets and redeploy them to enhance shareholder values. According to this report, in 1986 some 4,000 of America's largest companies would spend nearly $200 billion to transform themselves. This includes USX, the successor to US Steel, the first $1 billion corporation founded by J.P. Morgan in 1901.

Merger-mania is also invading the banking world, led by

Citicorp, whose $186 billion in assets make it America's largest bank. *U.S.News* (Nov. 24, '86, 49) claims that the U.S. "is in the midst of a defacto interstate-banking binge," despite the existence of federal laws designed to outlaw multi-state banks. In 1981, the nation's 15,000 banks, with a few exceptions, were limited to their home states by a federal law prohibiting their operation across state lines unless otherwise permitted by individual states. Congress has regularly rejected pleas to drop the barrier.

To circumvent this law, the banks have gone directly to the state legislatures and this strategy has produced a drastic change. Now thirty-six states and Washington D.C. have approved some form of interstate banking and the race is on. Regional banks in the Northeast, Southeast, Midwest and West are creating new conglomerates to operate across state lines. Some of the largest banks, like New York's Chase Manhattan and Citicorp, have gotten their feet in the doors of several states by buying troubled thrifts and savings and loan associations. *U.S. News* reports that now Citicorp is supposedly exploring methods of acquiring Bank-America, even though this California institution is technically off limits to any New York bank.

The new system of automated tellers is adding further fuel to this fire. It is reported that more than 70 percent of the nation's 64,000 teller machines are linked to national telecommunications systems like Cirrus or Plus. Customers can withdraw cash or check their account balances at machines across the country. State boundaries are becoming more academic than real and the old laws don't seem adequate to deal with this new computerized society.

Beyond the technological changes and the immediate struggle for survival, what seems to be happening at a deeper level is a massive challenge to America's traditional restrictions on trusts and monopolies in the name of corporate profit. The government's response seems to be a general relaxation in restraining business at this point. This has been a long-standing battle. Our opposition to monopolies traces back through the

Clayton anti-trust act of 1914 and the Sherman act of 1890 to
the British anti-monopoly act of 1624, the prohibitions against
monopolies in Roman law, and finally back to the Old Testament where Isaiah condemns the Hebrews "who add field to
field until there is no room." (5:8) George C.S. Benson, in his
book *Business Ethics in America*, states the problem exactly.
The anti-trust laws are clear. Monopolies are illegal. But the
U.S. has not yet succeeded in establishing anti-trust laws as a
basic ethical value. When you don't want to obey them, there
are many ways to get around the laws. Ultimately, it is an
ethical question dealing with the spirit as well as the letter of
the law.

This is usually argued out on a tactical level. The case for
conglomerates has been forcefully made by George J. Benson
in his book *Conglomerate Mergers*. These are often an investment for the acquiring company, preferable to paying out more
dividends, or putting more money into an industry that already
has under-utilized capacity. Smaller companies are often glad
to be merged for a variety of reasons. Mergers may bring about
important economies such as joint warehousing and shipping
or savings in research and development. They also usually
result in diversified cash flow and permit the acquisition of
unusual talent and the displacement of poor managers. Benson
claims that conglomerates are likely to increase competition
through the reinvigoration of the acquired companies. He argues that the growth of economic and political power as a
result of such mergers is not alarming. As the special report in
Business Week points out, economist Joseph A. Schumpeter
and those who follow him insist that the restructuring of corporate America is an inevitable and essentially healthy
response to new economic fundamentals. "The companies that
emerge from the rubble will be more efficient and competitive."

The other side of this tactical discussion is that mergers
and such elaborate restructuring often lead to the demise of an
industry. Corporations scout the country for healthy small
businesses which are ripe for take-over and then proceed to

dismember them, bleed them of their assets, and so destroy them. It doesn't really pay to be healthy anymore. Robert Howard, in an article in *The New Republic*, describes the case of Colonial Press of Clinton, Massachusetts. At its height, Colonial employed 1,750 people. Various mergers placed the company in the hands of first one, then another conglomerate. By this time, the work force was down to 800. Sheller-Globe, a Toledo-based automobile parts firm, had obtained Colonial almost by mistake because it was a subsidiary of the Victorine Corporation acquired by Sheller-Globe. With neither the interest nor ability to operate Colonial Press, Sheller-Globe, after refusing to sell the plant to the workers, auctioned off the plant machinery and shut it down.

George C. Benson argues that mergers, in fact, deplete a company's assets, do not generally result in increased productivity, endanger both the employees and the stockholders, and through questionable accounting methods make it seem like the conglomerate is making substantial income. But this does not have a solid economic base. Studies show that much of the existing management after a merger does not remain with the merged company. In 1972, Ralph Nader and others did a study showing that conglomerates, although at times helping competition, could also be anti-competitive. A study of the takeover of United Fruit Company by AMK conglomerate shows that everyone gained in the deal except the shareholders and the employees.

At A Deeper Level

At a superficial tactical level, the questions of expediency, efficiency and profit resulting from mergers will no doubt continue to be argued out among the various participants. Our greater concern here is for the deeper level of ethical strategy. From a Hebrew-Christian standpoint, the major issues raised by restructuring and mergers are those of freedom and social responsibility. Do these tactics seriously curtail the freedom of the industry in particular or the economy in general? The charge of restraint of trade is still an important ethical concern: freedom is necessary to the operation of an economy reflecting the justice of God.

Do they permit a concern for persons and communities and for the long-term effect upon the larger industry or society in general? The justice of God requires the operation of love in the social and corporate situation. In economic terms, this translates into a concern that puts persons ahead of profits, the general welfare ahead of that of an individual corporation. It is interested in lost jobs, human anguish and the destruction of communities when plants are moved about like pawns on a chessboard.

Norman Jaspan has headed a firm which locates employee crime. His conclusion after decades of experience is that mergers foster disloyalty. He points to one construction firm, taken over by a conglomerate, where the managers simply milked the company for all they could get, and then disappeared. In another case, an executive of twenty-five years service was downgraded because of a merger. He retaliated by setting up his own business, using the company's dies, equipment and personnel.

When a firm ceases to care for its personnel, it creates an unjust situation, and the result is almost inevitably the downward spiral of frustration, cynicism, dishonesty and some kind of violence. Raines and Day-Lower point to the loss of morale among workers at the Eaton plant that closed in Philadelphia. As one worker put it, "once the plant closes they lose all faith in everything." The cost to communities and the hardening of individual consciences from the doing of violence to individuals cannot be calculated on a balance sheet.

The problem of the merger-mania is the problem of greed. When the legitimate self-interest of a corporation operates without the restraints of a concern for the workers and the communities that sustain them, then self-interest has become greed because it has become unjust. The pattern seems to be that industry will use its power to gain special concessions in market competition, leading to monopoly capitalism. The assumption of Adam Smith that self-interest among consumers, when combined with competition among producers, will transform individual greed into the fuel of an efficient economy is being challenged today by the runaway inflation of corporate mergers and the trail of wreckage they leave behind. Private greed, it would appear, does not necessarily produce public good because greed is self-interest out of control.

Outsourcing

One of the most dramatic responses of industry to the current threats to its survival has been that of moving plants overseas, what is called outsourcing. This is to take advantage of the low wages, tax incentives and freedom from unions and U.S. government regulation. The U.S. Bureau of Economic Analysis in 1970 surveyed 298 U.S. firms operating overseas. Sperry Lea and Simon Webley defined this more strictly in 1973 as about 200 multinational corporations based in the United States, out of 300 worldwide. According to this study, "strictly speaking, MNCs comprise only a relatively few of the swelling number of firms operating internationally."

This growth has taken place within what Robert Howard, in *The New Republic* has called "Runaway Plants," some of which have moved to other parts of America while others have moved overseas. In 1950, it is reported that 5 per cent of total invested capital had moved overseas. By 1972, it had increased to 10 per cent, and the volume continues to rise, severely contracting the domestic job market. Braybrooke points to Cornell economists Robert Frank and Richard Freeman who place the net job loss between 1966 and 1973, at 1.6 million, with 735,000 in industry alone. While manufacturing employment in the U.S. dropped by 3 per cent between 1967 and 1976, the decrease in the northeast and north-central regions was 13 per cent, representing nearly 1.5 million jobs. This is equal to all the manufacturing jobs available in Ohio in 1969. For whatever reason, in Ohio over 150,000 jobs have been lost since 1973. This industrial hemorrhage continues, most recently with the movement out of state of both Goodyear and Goodrich tire and rubber plants.

A classic case in point involves the General Electric plant in Ontario, California. This facility had manufactured irons for many years, and was one of the main foundations of Ontario's economy. The problem was that the plant was making only 4 per cent profit, and the management decided that at least 6 per cent was necessary to stay in business. The decision was to turn to the manufacture of cheaper plastic irons, and do it in Brazil, Mexico and Singapore. The workers attempted various means to keep the plant open, but to no avail. It was closed. Despite some last minute efforts on the part of G.E. to help its workers find new jobs, the damage to individuals and to the community was severe.

Whether or not G.E. could have saved the situation by continuing in Ontario is a tactical question only those involved could answer. Our concern here is more with the ethical strategy questions that are raised by this example of what is becoming an increasingly familiar pattern. The ethical truth is that tactics and strategy go together. The ends tend to take on the quality of the means which are used. If the means are unjust, then eventually the final product will be unjust and will not work. If the Hebrew-Christian ethic is to be believed, profit is a by-product of a commitment to ethical values.

The basic question is one of social justice, for a corporation is an intensely social entity. In many ways, it represents the most influential and characteristic social institution of our day. This suggests that the ethical strategies applying to society are especially applicable to corporations. In a Hebrew-Christian context, this becomes a matter of the priority of the quality of life over the quantity of profit, the recognition that under the sovereignty of a God of justice long-range considerations take precedence over short-range expediency, that human relationships are more important than the bottom line of a balance sheet. Translated into economic terms, this suggests that a strong concern for the human dimension is, in fact, the best business. Justice, from this theological standpoint, is an exercise in corporate love. The love that reflects the justice of God is concerned to make the good life possible for all. People must know that if they work nobly and sacrificially and do their best, there will be appropriate reward for their faithfulness. Without that assurance, human morale degenerates and the downward spiral of cynicism, dishonesty and violence results.

Raines and Day-Lower point out that is exactly why taking work out of laboring class communities is so unfair. "It takes away not just paychecks but something far more important. It takes away the means of defending dignity. It attacks the workers' values that support their community and their personal identity." Studies continue to show that the most successful corporations are those which foster the pride and dignity of all their personnel, both labor and management. To ignore this is to place oneself and one's corporation under the judgment of God's wrath. The danger is that in the frenzied tactics of survival this fundamental truth will be lost. Lasting, healthy profit is a by-product of a situation that reflects the justice of God.

Corporate justice demands a very broad concern involving what Eugene Beem, Professor of Business Ethics at Baldwin Wallace College, calls the "stakeholder model." The corporate organization involves not only shareholders, but customers, management, labor and society in general. A successful corporation is one where the interests of all are in proper balance. The problem of greed arises when profit for the shareholders becomes the over-riding concern to the exclusion of the rest.

There have been some efforts to legislate a solution to the problem of outsourcing. Bills are pending in many states which would force corporations to bear the social cost of their moving, costs which are now largely borne by the workers and the communities. The principle is ethically sound. A corporation is a community. As such, it has a right to move when that is a truly corporate decision, and when the cost is borne by the corporation itself. But no corporate entity has the moral right to improve its own situation at the expense of others who are neither part of it, nor have had any say in the decision. Paraphrasing John Donne, "no corporation is an island." We are all part of the same social continent. A corporation must act responsibly within the community just as individuals must do.

The New Vision of a Global Village

One of the most fascinating developments in the drama of outsourcing is a heightened awareness of our global interdependence. The question which thoroughly complicates the picture is whether or not our over-riding concern for the success of American industry is compatible with the Hebrew-Christian ethic or with the realities of our situation. John Naisbitt, in his book *Megatrends,* documents the shift in America from a self-sufficient national economy to being part of an interdependent global economy. We are being forced to give up our former role as the world's dominant power and recognize that we are only one member of a growing handful of economically strong countries, including many newcomers like Taiwan, South Korea, Hong Kong, Mexico and Brazil. According to Naisbitt, by the year 2000, the Third World countries will manufacture 30 per cent of the world's goods. Whether we like it or not, we are becoming more and more part of an economic fabric that ties us to the rest of the world. This means that in new ways that are being daily explored the success of American industry is bound to the success of industry throughout the global village.

The ethical question here is one of American chauvinism and isolationism. It has to do with the stature of our love for others and the extent of our vision of global justice. The demands for protectionist tariffs carry weight if they are made in the name of fairness and justice. But if they are merely an effort to preserve American world dominance, then they lose their ethical integrity. The criticism of industry for moving overseas has force if done in the name of the economic welfare of American workers and of the quality of life in American communities torn apart by such disruption. But if these objections are raised in the name of preserving an inflated wage scale, and an over-extended lifestyle, then they lose their convincing power.

The fact is that most of the world is living in the kind of poverty experienced by very few in this country. The availability of cheap overseas labor, which prompts the problem of outsourcing in the first place, makes this plain. America has been an island of plenty in a vast sea of want. It may very well be that the economic necessities of our situation are forcing us to realize that our extravagant standard of living can no longer be justified either economically or ethically. Outsourcing would seem to be a symptom of a global economic readjustment that is as inevitable as it is long overdue. The South Korean who makes electronic goods to be sold under the trade name of Sears, J.C. Penney and Sylvania is, in a curious way, forcing us to rediscover not only some of the laws of economics, but of social justice as well.

Fraud and Deception

Jesus criticized the leaders of his day for their greed and lack of concern for justice and righteousness and called them "children of hell." It is a painfully attested ethical fact that injustice is an open door to the downward plunge into the hell of cynicism, dishonesty and some form of death. Greed is economic injustice. Throughout this study so far we will see that at every point where greed is especially concentrated there is an outbreak of dishonesty. This is evident today in the corporate scene as the desperate efforts of industry to survive have prompted the escalation of fraud and white collar crime.

If greed is one of the main motivators in the surge of white collar crime, nowhere is this more sensitive than in the corporate sector where the fortunes of the business community are tightly bound together. A classic case in point involves the collapse of E.S.M. Government Securities, Inc. of Fort Lauderdale, Florida. Founded in 1976, for a decade the company had shown its customers a healthy balance, certified by a Chicago firm of auditors. It offered investors high interest rates for short-term loans backed by U.S. Government securities. In order to operate, the firm required a continuing and substantial inflow of securities and cash, much of it provided by financial institutions controlled by Marvin Warner, owner of Home State Savings Bank of Cincinnati. It appears that the withdrawal by another bank of securities which E.S.M. could not cover began the chain of events leading to its undoing. After its collapse in 1985, the S.E.C. charged that E.S.M had concealed some $196.5 million in accumulated losses. How this was done is a puzzle which has taken a long time to sort out.

E.S.M's two largest customers were The American Savings and Loan Association of Florida and Warner's Home State bank. American's customers lost about $300 million, and Home State closed its doors, which rocked the entire savings and loan industry. Ohio was the hardest hit. Governor Richard Celeste was forced to declare a three day bank holiday for 71 savings and loan associations in what was called the most extensive closure of U.S. financial institutions since the Great Depression. Communities from Beaumont, Texas, to Pompano Beach, Florida, were badly shaken. The upshot of this disaster was that the Ohio legislature had to pass special legislation to stem the run on state S&Ls. Marvin Warner, former ambassador to Switzerland, was sentenced to three and a half years in prison. It cost the state of Ohio an estimated $226 million to settle losses and stabilize the situation. (*New York Times*, March 14, '85; *Time*, March 25, '85, 57) Since then, it has become apparent that so many S&Ls have gone bankrupt the FSLIC can't bail them out. Taxpayers will have to pay the bill, variously estimated from $50 to $100 billion. In a report on this matter by MacNeil-Lehrer (10/18/88), all agreed that one significant cause was the amount of fraud and dishonesty within this industry.

Harry Girvetz, in his book *Contemporary Moral Issues*, calls what we are experiencing "a moral crisis," with honesty the prime issue. The evidence continues to accumulate. General Dynamics recently replaced its president following the indictment of three officers who were having "ethical problems." The new president, Stanley Pace, was appointed, according to a prominent CEO and longtime friend, primarily to get them out of the ethical mess into which they had fallen. *The Wall Street Journal* detailed the charges that General Dynamics repeatedly violated federal laws and regulations by improperly billing the government for expenses and by providing expensive gifts and entertainment for high ranking military officials. Although claiming that the media had misrepresented and exaggerated the facts, the ousted president did admit that "in hindsight, there have been some mistakes made ...we have found some cases that look very wrong to us...a great deal of work to do...in justifying bills submitted to the government." After three years, it has been reported that the government is giving up the investigation because it didn't think it could win in the courts due to lack of evidence.

The trail of dishonesty is a long one, and the Greed Syndrome operates throughout. Douglas Bauer, reporting in *New York Times Magazine* (March 8, '81), quotes David Joys of the Russell Reynolds Consulting Firm in New York City:

"I know...we all know...of people all over this town who are running their companies into the ground, taking huge, quick profits and leaving them a shell. And when you look at their contracts it's easy to see why. What does it matter to them what happens ten years from now? They're building giant personal fortunes, and appear to be running their companies terrifically, and in ten years, when there's nothing left, they'll be long gone."

The May 15, '87 issue of *Time* continues this litany with an impressive collection of white collar scams where greed combined with technology has made stealing more tempting than ever. "The decade of the entrepreneur is becoming the age of the pinstriped outlaw." Some of this is blatant thievery, like the savings and loan officers in Texas, all with large salaries, who loot their own business to purchase Rolls-Royces and trips to Paris, or like TRW over-charging the Pentagon for fighter plane parts. Some cases are more subtle, like the many indictments for tax evasion, or illegal tax shelter promotion. Other cases are more ethically complex, like Manville's huge asbestos output or A.H. Robin's Dalkon shield intrauterine device, both declared hazards to health, or the charge that Ford refused to do anything about the fuel tank of its Pintos even after company engineers told them the placement of the fuel tank increased the risk of fatal rear-end accidents. (*Harper's*, Dec. '82, 40)

Labor is also much involved in this apparent lowering of ethical morale within the corporate sector. Raines and Day-Lower report from their research the widespread attitudes among workers that they are merely passive consumers of paychecks rather than active participants in a productive effort. The "I-don't-live-here-I-just-work-here" attitude common among some workers reveals an alienation from their work. This reflects a lowering of morale and often results in an increase in dishonesty as an almost inevitable product of the absence of some aspect of justice within the system. It was reported to me, for example, that the union employees of a prominent china factory in Ohio contracted to pile only so many plates each hour, after which they would play cards until it was again time to pile their quota. The company has since lost its market to the Japanese who still have an Oriental version of the Protestant work ethic. We are being forced to re-discover the meaning of quality within American industry which is closely tied to the old concept of "an honest day's work."

The oft-reported domination of some unions by the Mafia, if true, would be one of the most sinister evidences of the loss of a concern for honesty within this segment of American industry. If workers felt that their rights were being ignored and their dignity challenged through inadequate wages, or if they were treated as non-entities by management, then the downward spiral of injustice would begin, with lowered morale, cynicism, dishonesty, and usually some form of violence. This would make them highly vulnerable to an invasion by organized crime.

The question arises as to how serious the problem of dishonesty is within either management or labor. Without question, most Americans operate with a reasonable measure of honesty and many are dedicated to it. The question is, how widespread is dishonesty? Is it increasing? Is it affecting the national economy? Is it a sickness unto death? My information tells me that it is indeed increasing and is having a damaging effect on our economy. Others would, no doubt, disagree. That it is a sickness unto death would be harder to dispute.

The Corporate Greed Syndrome

But now let's look below the surface of these disturbing symptoms. The real revolution we are going through is one of ethical strategies which lie behind these various responses of corporate America to the threats to its survival. The driving motivation seems to be that immediate profit takes precedence over the concerns of morality, persons and society. This is the logic of expediency. For example, Benson points to the major cause behind the ethical problems of Westinghouse as top management "piling on the pressure" for profits without monitoring how they were made. (*Business Ethics in America*, 159) This is an economic adaptation of the same attitude recently surfacing in the Iran-Contra affair and helps to explain the origin of some of the things we are describing.

The "Invisible Hand"

Another basic strategy involves the revival of Adam Smith and his philosophy of the "invisible hand," along with the application of Darwin's theory of evolution to social problems, sometimes called "economic darwinism." Just leave the economy alone and it will adjust itself due to the inherent laws of supply and demand. This philosophy is valid as far as it goes, but ultimately it is inadequate as a description of the nature of reality, for it ignores the justice of God. The law of the survival of the fittest is the brutal, impersonal law of the jungle, derived from the observation of plants and animals. But we are humans and, in the Hebrew-Christian ethical context, that makes all the difference. The problem is that, like the laws of evolution, it takes time for these economic laws to operate. In the meantime, many persons fall through the cracks. This impersonal indifference to the fate of others is a common source and symptom of the syndrome of greed we are describing.

The justice of God is more than the application of impersonal laws of nature or economics. It is the application of the moral laws of love. It is God's affirmation of our humanity and the freedom he gives us to make essential choices. We are not the victims of blind chance or inexorable natural or economic law because we are humans. As such, we are moral creatures capable of changing our physical or social environment and therefore responsible for each other and to God. There is an implied atheism in this rigid application of Adam Smith which modern economists should ponder carefully as they return in their supply-side enthusiasm to the doctrine of the invisible hand.

The Casuistry of Business Ethics

There is another ethical strategy lying behind the symptoms we have been reviewing. That is what Vincent Barry has called the casuistry of business ethics. This is the adaptation of personal and social responsibility to the demands of a particular situation. It often starts out as highly idealistic, like the situation ethics espoused by theologian Joseph Fletcher a generation ago. But as the testing of the intervening years has clearly shown, an ethic so thoroughly dependent on the situation regularly ends up being merely an exercise in the expediency of self-interest. There is ethical validity in paying close attention to the necessities of a particular situation, especially as they reflect the needs of those involved. But the problem comes when escalating self-interest unites with the denial of any ethical absolutes. This produces the kind of attitude so prevalent today which has been the principal ethical justification for the Greed Syndrome. Right and wrong are to be decided by each individual unhindered by any over-riding ethical necessities. Ethical chaos describes our current situation.

The Thoreau Syndrome

An extension of this attitude comes from what has been called "the Thoreau Syndrome." Henry David Thoreau, an eighteenth century New England rebel-man of letters-devotee of forests and lakes, in his "Essay on Civil Disobedience," gave an eloquent case for disobeying the laws that he didn't agree with. He was widely read by college students in the 1960s, and in many ways set the tone for the attitudes and lifestyles of that decade. Although the manner of living has changed since the 1960s, the attitude lingers on. If we don't agree with the law, we are justified, yea, even sanctified, by disobeying it. The thing at stake here is the rule of law, certainly one of the foundations of a democracy. The example set by some corporations, presidents, government agencies and even churches is merely a reflection of the widespread influence of this form of antinomianism (opposition to law). It often begins with high idealism, like defending one's country or saving one's business; but when united with the pressures of self-interest, this easy attitude toward the law can quickly become a firestorm of greed.

Ethical Strategies for Corporate Success

The question, then, is what makes for a successful corporation? I wouldn't presume to advise corporate executives on the tactics of successful management. My thesis is an ethical one. Managerial success is a by-product of many deeper ethical and religious concerns. The really crucial question then becomes, how can we make a just profit? What is the meaning of profit integrity? Raines and Day-Lower point to the crackpot realism of corporations which ignore the kinds of ethical concerns to which we have been pointing while mortgaging their future and inviting destruction through policies of short-term expediency. One of the greatest corporate needs of this day is to rediscover the ethical values that founded this country in the first place and have maintained whatever stability we have had through the years. The growing chorus of those who are making this point includes a wide range of persons: corporate executives and ethics professors, Jews and Christians, believers and non-believers.

Within the Hebrew-Christian tradition, the only unassailable absolute that transcends all individuals and all situations is the sovereignty and justice of God. If there is a God, and if he resembles the God of the Bible, then surely it is here that we should look for ethical strategies and tactics that define in more exact detail an ethical program for corporate success that has some chance of embracing us all in this pluralistic society.

The Hebrew-Christian ethic is not a code with a list of do's and don'ts, although the Ten Commandments have indeed acted as a convenient summary and lowest common denominator. This ethic is a way of life that reflects the sovereignty and justice of God in all the ways we act, think and feel, penetrating to the heart of our greed and self-deception. It aims at causes as well as symptoms, at therapy as well as diagnosis, at guidance as well as criticism. Translated into economic terms, although not a code, it can become a series of ethical strategies or principles from which tactical decisions can be derived. Many of these have already surfaced in this study.

1. The sovereignty of God demands that we place God first, others second, and our own personal concern for profit last in our list of priorities. The best business is one that puts abiding values and service to others ahead of the maximization of profits.

2. Under the sovereignty of God, the concerns of the long range take precedence over those of immediate expediency. The solid, genuine success of a corporation is a product of its concern for the future and for the wider community.

3. God's loving justice is concerned to provide appropriate rewards for righteousness. In economic terms, this means that if labor or management work faithfully and do their best, then salary, working conditions, job security and provision for the future will reflect the corporate appreciation of such integrity. There is no better formula for corporate success. The opposite, according to Raines and Day-Lower, is to shatter the American dream and produce the toxins that poison a corporation and a society.

4. God's love requires that we provide sources of help for individuals and institutions that make the good life possible. For corporations, this suggests training programs for the upward movement of management or labor, aid to individuals and families in the form of medical insurance, incentive bonuses, financial assistance and various helps to individuals and communities devastated by plant closings or removals.

5. God's wrath demands restraint on the sinful natures of men and women because we are constructed by nature to serve our own interests. This suggests a system of monitoring not only how well people do their work, but how ethically they do it. It also suggests a clear code of restraint so that both management and labor know what things are outside the bounds of company policy.

6. God's justice demands punishment for sin. Without it, there cannot be a just, and so a successful corporation. Corporations need to provide their own means of punishing anyone from the janitor to the CEO for unethical behavior.

7. The rule of law is an expression of God's justice. This

translates into the need for industries to set up the rules of the game as they see it. These then must be enforced, for without adequate enforcement we invite the downward spiral of cynicism, dishonesty and violence.

8. The condition of God's justice demands freedom to sin or to do good, to succeed or to fail. Within the corporate scene, this requires the freedom of both management and labor to make choices about their own behavior, to have a say in the policies of management, to be free from the tyranny of overbearing bosses, to have a personal stake in the quality of the product. The Japanese are showing us what many corporations already know: this kind of shared management is the very best way to insure corporate success.

9. Freedom must be exercised within an environment of law and restraint for it to be just. Otherwise it becomes license and is destructive instead of creative. One of the most important economic applications of this theological-ethical principle has to do with the current revival of laissez-faire economics. Freedom in the market place is important and it would seem that there are indeed economic laws that operate automatically, just as there are physical laws that do the same. But with economics, we are dealing with people who have enough intelligence to think creatively, and this means the ability to sin and go against their own best interests. Self-interest so quickly produces greed and all the products of injustice that attend it that economic freedom must be under constant surveillance and restraint.

10. The Apostle Paul adds another guideline that can have application to the corporate scene. He urges us to grow up in every way, into what he calls the maturity and stature of Jesus Christ. In economic terms, this suggests that companies are either growing or they are dying; but the growth that is needed is not just in corporate assets or volume of sales or cash on a balance sheet. The key to this ethical principle is the phrase "in every way." We are talking about the total ethical growth of a corporation in terms of its comprehensive quality. This must include profits, but it must also include ethical, social, personal

growth at every point. The exclusive fixation on profits is a formula for corporate death. There may be apparent, superficial gains in a corporation living only for the short run; but ultimately, inexorably, these moral laws of God's universe will bring it down.

Maturity In Love As Ethical Tactic

We need now to take a look at a positive program of ethical tactics that is true to the Hebrew-Christian ethic. Jesus gave the clue in his summary of the Old Testament law and the prophets: "Love the Lord your God with all your heart and with all your soul and with all your strength, and your neighbor as yourself." (Mark 12:28-34) The Apostle Paul extended this ethical summary in his concept of growing to maturity in love. (Eph. 4:13) The key word is love and this is expressed in three directions: to God, to neighbor and, lastly, to self. This would, I take it, apply to corporations as well as to individuals.

Within this threefold set of relationships, there are three activities which guide the tactical apprehension and application of the love of God. These three steps that lead to maturity on every level are actually first principles of modern clinical psychology as they are of good pedagogy and the scientific method. The first is loving God, others, and self with all your mind. This means we must *understand* God and others and self as accurately as possible. Not as we would have them be in some kind of arbitrary way, but exactly as they really are. If the Bible really is an adequate revelation of the person and nature of God, this is where we must begin for a discussion of ethics. It means that corporations must make a serious effort to define their goals and beliefs. These could be religious or philosophical or purely economic, but their ultimate ideology needs to be understood. Then they must understand themselves, their strengths and weaknesses, their hidden agendas, their hangups. This takes a degree of honesty that is difficult for everyone and especially for those in positions of authority. They must also understand each other in the total set of relationships that make up a corporation: stockholders, consumers, competitors, the communities in which they reside, the national interest. This takes a degree of open communication that is often difficult to achieve, but absolutely essential to a mature company.

The second act of a mature relationship is that of *accepting* one's ideology, one's neighbors and one's self on terms which are true to each. We must allow ideologies and principles and people and ourselves to be themselves whether we like them or not. We must begin a mature relationship with this kind of honest realism which prevents us from distorting ideas or persons or relationships or the simple facts of our situation. It does not mean we cannot work to improve all of this as we see it. But it does demand the basic acceptance of the fact that this is the way things are and that is what we are dealing with. So much of social failure is a product of living in an unreal world, unwilling to accept things and people as they are and to love them enough to let them be themselves.

This is an almost magical formula for opening up the best in every situation and it leads to the third step in a mature relationship: to *express* our ideologies, our associates, ourselves, our particular situation as best we can within the understanding and acceptance of who and what we are. Understanding, acceptance, and expression are the three tactical dimensions of maturity whether religious, ethical or corporate.

Maturity In Love and the Tactics of Corporate Success

The modern corporation is an intensely social entity. It is the peculiar invention of democratic capitalism and, as such, a microcosm of American society. Michael Novak points out that in this country there are two million economic corporations reporting to the IRS, plus approximately fifteen million small businesses, with about 100 million persons in the total work force. According to *Fortune* magazine, the largest corporation is General Motors, with 839,000 employees, followed by Ford with 506,531 and GE with 401,000. (Novak, *Toward a Theology of the Corporation*, 15) Peter Drucker, writing in *Forbes* (Sept. 14, 1981), makes it clear "that virtually all the concerns of 'business ethics'...have to do with relationships of interdependence, whether that between the organization and the employee, the manufacturer and the customer..."

Thus corporate management is an exercise in social ethics. It is no surprise, then, that Peters and Waterman, writing about excellence in business management, insist that the best companies pay explicit attention to values: "any organization in order to survive and achieve success, must have a sound set of beliefs on which it premises all its policies and actions." (*In Search of Excellence*, 280) They go on to outline the dominant beliefs of the most excellent companies: a belief in being the best, in the importance of the details of execution, in the importance of people as individuals, in superior quality and service; a belief that most members of the organization should be innovators, a belief in the importance of informality to enhance communication and, only lastly, an explicit belief in the importance of economic growth and profits.

In a curious way this list of values summarizes what we have been saying about the justice of God and maturity in love as applied to corporate industry. This same theme is reiterated by John Naisbitt and Patricia Aberdene in their book *Reinventing the Corporation*. The basic assumption of a re-invented company is that people are its most important asset: "people are profits." Self-management is replacing managers of people. Small team models, such as those used by Apple Computer, are a widespread alternative to bureaucratic organization. They cite IBM creating a version of the small team structure, independent business units, to fight its own bureaucratic tendencies. Their list of six characteristics of the ideal new-style company includes an environment for personal growth, managers as facilitators, not know-it-all experts, compensation systems based on performance, stock purchase plans, profit sharing and employee ownership, greater reliance on networking which is learning from one's peers, an opportunity for "intrapreneurs," that is, new ventures within the company, and lastly an emphasis on quality of life. In these new types of companies, the value system of the Hebrew-Christian ethic is clear. If they will indeed operate this way, then they will come close to reflecting the justice of God in their operation and will have the best possible chance to succeed.

One Case In Point

One of the modern success stories comes from the small college town of Wooster, Ohio, in a corporation begun two generations ago by a man of ethical integrity selling plastic dust pans door-to-door. Today, Rubbermaid is an international corporation, voted in 1987 as the third most attractive company in the nation. Don Noble, former CEO, attributes the success of Rubbermaid largely to their concern for moral integrity, clearly stated and aggressively followed. "The best way to maximize long range profit is to put abiding values and service to others as top priority." The election of the present CEO, Stanley Gault, to be President of the National Association of Manufacturers is further testimony by the economic community to their high regard for this corporation. Corporate success and ethical integrity do indeed go together. The best of the corporate world in many ways is ahead of the rest of American society in this regard despite the escalating inroads of the Greed Syndrome.

I include a summary of Rubbermaid's fundamental principles as an example of an impressive concern for the Hebrew-Christian ethic within one of America's most successful corporations:

RUBBERMAID FUNDAMENTAL PRINCIPLES

We believe in a single standard of conduct which will at all times consider the best long-term interests of the corporation, its stockholders, its employees, its customers, its suppliers, and the communities in which it operates. We believe that our customers, investors, employees, suppliers, and communities are entitled to share in the economic benefit created by our concerted effort to develop, produce, and market products of recognized value and utility. To this end we will strive,

For Our Customers
- to offer products of high quality and true value that incorporate leadership in design and utility.
- to work continuously and diligently to increase our knowledge of our customers and their requirements and to provide prompt and effective response to their needs.
- to work with our customers consistently, with honesty and integrity, and without discrimination.

For Our Investors
- to provide an acceptable return on investment.
- to maintain a program of sound growth supported by the profitable reinvestment of retained earnings balanced with a consistent dividend policy.
- to communicate the activities and performance of the Company on an effective and timely basis.
- to provide the competence and depth in our management organization necessary to develop and plan for effective utilization of the Company's resources to meet present and future corporate objectives.

For Our Employees
- to recognize the intrinsic value of each employee as an individual.
- to provide a working environment that encourages self-motivation and initiative.

- to offer equal opportunity for career growth and advancement within the Company based upon individual ability and demonstrated performance.
- to provide continuity of employment and fair rewards for job performance.

For Our Suppliers

- to establish and maintain mutually beneficial, long-term relationships which will result in maximum ultimate value to Rubbermaid for each dollar expended.
- to be equitable, and to operate with integrity.
- to be objective, and base purchases on value received, avoiding favors, gifts, or personal gratuities which would hamper independence of action.

For Our Communities

- to conduct business in an ethical and responsible manner.
- to support the economy and general welfare of the community whenever feasible and consistent with sound management practices.
- to encourage our employees to participate in community affairs.
- to encourage our employees to assume civic responsibilities in active support of the kind of government which will maintain and promote the private enterprise system.

Needed: A Higher Ethical Profile

It is no accident that in their book, *In Search of Excellence*, Peters and Waterman place shared values at the heart of their model for corporate success. The problem is that this kind of ethical concern is not something one can legislate except in specific cases. Even then there is always a way to cheat. The increase in the production of ethical codes within industry is an encouraging thing, but the key lies deeper. It is a matter of a consciousness and a motivation that must be raised within the secret recesses of individual minds whence come the tactics that will make or break our society. Our best defense against the Greed Syndrome is a public attitude that sees this as an ethical matter, puts a clear label on what is being done, and rallies those with high-minded concern to create an ethical climate in which this disease can no longer flourish.

But we are reluctant to speak out on ethical matters. Peters and Waterman report that while most CEOs believe in the importance of ethics in business, they are reluctant to say much about it. Rubbermaid's Don Noble comments on Earl Cheit's article in the *Cleveland Plain Dealer*, giving advice to Stanley Pace, the new CEO of General Dynamics, hired to restore its ethical credibility. Cheit urged Pace to "resist the temptation to start by issuing a code of ethics." In a letter to Pace, Noble strongly disagreed: "I think that is exactly where you should start. A code of ethics would announce early your intention to reward ethical behavior and to punish unethical behavior."

What seems to be needed is some clarity on these matters, to develop a theologically sophisticated business ethic, and to get the total business community out of the closet in its ethical concerns.

Chapter 6

I Want to Make a Killing

"'The bad apple speeches are crap...This (Boesky) case is illustrative of the general wretched excess on the street. The line between what's right and wrong has been blurred. This is Wall Street's Watergate.'" "The Street," as it is called, is much in the news these days. As this quote from an investment banker in *Newsweek* (Dec. 1, '86, 49) indicates, the issues seem to be as much ethical as they are economic. The shift of our profit-making center to a dual economy where investment banking is challenging corporate industry for dominance has opened up fabulous possibilities for good or evil. The problem is, which is which, and where do you draw the line?

Some are insisting that this is just the rediscovery of the very old system of merchant banking, so successful in late medieval Europe, as American business learns new ways of operating on a national and global scale. Others are pointing to the amorality of Wall Street where economic terrorism is the norm and the only rule is to stay just within the law, or don't get caught. The parallel with the days of the so-called "Robber Barons" following the Civil War is striking. Only the names and scenarios have changed. Instead of Jay Gould and the Erie Railroad Gang, we now have Ivan Boesky and the Wall Street crowd. Then it was railroads and the winning of the West. Now the new frontier is investment banking and an economy feeding upon itself. Then it was "Go west, young man." Today the cry is "invest, young men and women." There are some new questions, but basically the same unchecked greed that fueled those corporate pirates of old now motivates the stockmarketeers of today. And we are confused. It would seem that if you take enough, stealing isn't so bad. Luxury jails, short sentences and $100 million fines are not a bad price to pay for making a billion.

Aside from the question as to whether it is good for the nation's economy, this exotic appearance of the Greed Syndrome has raised again in new ways an entire generation of ethical questions dealing with white collar crime, the fastest growing criminal phenomenon in the nation: the separation of legality from justice, the balancing of freedom and restraint, the relation of long-range to short-range policies, the responsibility of clever men and women to others as they fatten themselves on the fruits of this over-abundant land.

The Hebrew-Christian ethic has much to say about these matters in terms of the justice and sovereignty of God and the Apostle Paul's concept of maturity in love. As far as I can see, it is only within such a powerful ethic that we have any real defense against the modern buccaneers who lie in wait for every fat merchantman who dares to sail these waters.

The Takeover War

Some liken it to a gigantic game of Monopoly, others call it a revolution, and still others a rash of economic terrorism. As the evidence piles up, it is more and more being seen as a full scale war, undeclared and yet total, for we are all involved whether we have enlisted or not. The antagonists are traditional industry and the American economy on the one hand, and a new and prodigiously aggressive breed of investment banker posing as Lone Ranger, Robin Hood, David battling Goliath, or Bluebeard the Pirate on the other. Andrew Sigler, in *U.S. News and World Report* (Dec. 1, '86, 51), calls the recent flood of hostile takeovers the handiwork of a new caste of professional raiders whose strategy is to wage blitzkrieg warfare devised to outflank the corporate board of directors and stampede the stockholders. "The outcome is a dismemberment of some of America's largest companies, an unhealthy increase in the amount of debt they carry, and damage to shareholders, employees and local communities."

By now, the media have well covered the lines of battle and the principal figures in the conflict. The chief prize seems to be the excess of cash available within the American economy. The comparison to the game of Monopoly is apt, except for the fact that the level of amorality and dedicated viciousness takes this out of the status of a parlor game. This is for real. The stakes are unbelievable wealth or financial disaster, fantastic power or personal ruin, a healthy economy or one crippled by the devastation of a war we didn't want or have anything to say about.

The plan of battle is to amass an impressive amount of money, either through the concentration of one's own assets, enlisting the aid of confederates, leveraging (which is pledging the assets of the targeted company as collateral for a loan), or through borrowing massive amounts of money from merchant bankers like Drexel, Burnham and Lambert, Merrill Lynch, and a host of others. These not only advise their customers as to the best investments in time-honored ways, but actually seek take-over opportunities and provide enormous sums of money, especially where profits can be expected to be quick and extravagant. It is often pointed out that the real drive for the takeover war comes from these investment banking houses who have captured the economic initiative from the more traditional corporations.

The tactics are to seek out public corporations with undervalued assets which can be turned into quick cash. Then one quietly buys up a controlling block of stock, or publicly threatens to do so, and either takes over the company and attempts to run it more efficiently, or sells it piecemeal for more than it was originally valued. Or one can sell the stock back to the terrified company at a sizeable profit, and walk away, often without ever having seen the beleaguered victim. This which is cynically called "greenmail" is really blackmail, but there is so much money involved that its color must surely be green.

The generals in this war are the large banking houses of Wall Street. The company commanders are some of the brightest, most aggressive, and, it turns out, unscrupulous money manipulators seen on the Street since the days of Jay Gould, Jim Fisk, and Daniel Drew. Michael Thomas, former investment banker and columnist for *The New York Times*, has called this undeclared economic war a mixture of a battlefield and a casino.

T. Boone Pickens was chosen by *Time* magazine (March 4, '85, 52f.) as the most famous and controversial of these battle-wise warriors. He is described as a prodigiously hard-working Texas maverick, overflowing with ideas, whose ability was unrecognized by his earlier bosses in the oil business. After knocking about the oil fields for a time, he formed an exploration company and was on his way. The heart of his fortune is Mesa Petroleum which he formed in 1964 and whose energy discoveries and lucrative investments by 1984 boosted sales to $413 million. In the early 1980s, riding the crest of the OPEC wave which tripled the price of oil, followed by a world oil glut after 1982, Pickens began drilling for oil on Wall Street, realizing that it was easier and more profitable to acquire oil by taking over oil companies than by actually drilling. Like a modern David, one of his first targets was the goliath Gulf Oil (1984 sales $284 billion) which he forced to sell out to Chevron in what was then called the biggest merger in business history. Pickens's profit was $760 million.

The question is, did Pickens emerge as a villain or a hero from his victorious battle with Gulf Oil? Wall Street immediately made him a hero, since its arbitrageurs walked away from their secondary speculation on the deal with $300 million. New York's Mayor Edward Koch gave him a crystal replica of the "Big Apple" in recognition of the $50 million the Gulf battle had brought to the city in fees for legal and other services. Shareholders welcomed the takeover because it jacked up their stock prices to dramatic new levels. He estimated that about 750,000 small investors saw the value of their holdings grow about $12 billion. In reviewing the mergers prompted by Pickens and other raiders, the President's Council of Economic Advisors, in its 1985 report said, "The available evidence is that mergers and acquisitions increase national wealth. They improve efficiency, transfer scarce resources to higher valued uses, and stimulate effective corporate management." More recently, however, Congress has been preparing federal legislation to curb hostile takeovers (*Dun's Business Month*, Feb. '87), suggesting that this initial estimate was naive and possibly as much a symptom of the problem as an aid to a solution.

Oil executives are less complimentary in objecting to Pickens's high-sounding idealism. Harold Hammer, Gulf executive vice-president who opposed him, is quoted to the effect that his only objection to Pickens "is the aura he tries to create when he says he is for the small shareholder." G.C. Richardson, retired executive of Cities Service, insists that "he's only after the almighty buck...nothing but a pirate." (*Time*, March 4, '85, 54) Clearly, Pickens caused a great deal of trouble and antagonism, distracted the corporation from running its business, and forced it and others to assume mountains of debt to conclude the battle.

Our question is an ethical one: How do you distinguish here between what is legal, efficient and "increases national wealth" and what is moral and truly good for the nation? Maybe there is no difference. It would seem to me to be a matter of deciding what kind of wealth we are looking for: cash flow for a limited few, or the personal and social well being of the total community.

Carl Icahn, another warrior in this conflict, is more candid. He freely admits that he is in the takeover game to make money. He did purchase TWA because he claimed it was undervalued and poorly managed. And he actually spent some time running it. But his main target seems to be the fast buck.

His raids on TWA, Philips Petroleum, USX and others appear to have been prompted not by public spirited concern or what he calls "outrage" at undervalued and inefficient companies, but by the large cash flow which is the blood scent to a financial tiger. According to *Newsweek* (Oct. 20, '86, 50f.), he sees himself as hunting tigers.

Phillips Petroleum has been a particularly tough opponent, first for Pickens, whose takeover bid in 1984 rallied the entire community, with local churches holding 24 hour prayer vigils to ward him off, and Pickens eventually losing $100 million on the attempt. Later, however, Icahn's raid on Phillips, although again repulsed by the spirited people of Bartlesville, Oklahoma, the company headquarters, netted the raider what *Newsweek* estimated to be about $35 million. Said Pickens: "I do it to make money...that's how I score in this game and those are the points...but you get a lot of satisfaction from correcting something you think is wrong."

Goodyear Is A Good Example

A classic case comes from the heartland of America. Sir James Goldsmith, a flamboyant, British-French jet-setting corporate raider made his fortune buying and selling large corporations. Goodyear, an 88-year-old institution with 133,000 employees in 28 countries, was on the list of corporations ripe for takeover. With the aid of Merrill Lynch, he managed to acquire 12.5 per cent of the Goodyear stock with sufficient funds available for buying them out. Goldsmith, who confessed he knew nothing about the tire business, calculated that the company could be subdivided and sold for a large profit, with Merrill Lynch making over $100 million on the deal.

The city of Akron responded like a community under military siege, with civic groups rushing to the defense of this industry which had for so many years provided much of its life blood. A delegation chartered busses and converged on Washington for a direct confrontation with Goldsmith who had been called to testify to Congress on his Akron raid. After hard lobbying by both sides, the Ohio legislature eventually passed legislation making it easier for Goodyear to protect itself from an unfriendly takeover. In most states, the statutes make clear that corporate directors have only one loyalty, and that is to the corporation and its shareholders. Ohio's new anti-takeover law made it legally possible for directors also to consider the interests of employees, suppliers, creditors, customers, the community, the state and national economy, and society in general in its decision. This makes such ethical sense that one wonders why it had to be legislated.

The second unusual provision in this new law says that in assessing takeover bids, directors shall consider "the long-term as well as the short-term interest of a corporation." Here is the "devil's ear" emerging from this legislative debate. The courts themselves had previously locked us into an economic value system which ignored any concern for long range benefit, and this midwestern legislature had the temerity to challenge its immortality.

The result was that Goldsmith and the directors of Goodyear struck a deal whereby Goodyear could buy back its stock at $49.50 a share, giving Goldsmith a profit of $94 million on a process that took 10 weeks, and did not even require a visit to Akron.

Goldsmith insisted that what he did was good for the corporation, making them more efficient by forcing them to divest themselves of subsidiary industries, like the making of blimps, and focusing more on the manufacture of tires. He argued that he was acting in the best interests of Akron and the American economy by unlocking between $2 billion and $3 billion in shareholder assets that the company's managers had not been properly exploiting. Goodyear's stock had been languishing at around $36 a share before the takeover bid, but after it the value rose to between $50 and $60 a share. The main criteria here would seem to be those of a cash standard value, quick profits, short term planning and a high degree of self-interest.

Goodyear and Akron, on the other hand, saw the benefits

in terms of a different set of criteria, involving more long-term, socially oriented standards. Goodyear was forced to sell its aerospace industry, and the Celeron oil and gas pipeline subsidiary, and abandon temporarily its long-range plans for growth through diversification. The price tag for bailing itself out would be a million a day on debt interest alone. Thousands of Goodyear workers, including more than 700 in Akron, would lose their jobs. The city itself would be fighting for its life for years to come.

Is all of this good for the economy, or only for Sir James Goldsmith, Merrill Lynch and a few shareholders? How one answers these questions depends on his or her standards of value. San Francisco historian Kevin Starr complained in a memorial statement: "people don't get rich (today) by putting people to work, but by putting people out of work." (*Newsweek* Dec. 1,'86, 49)

The special edition of *The Beacon Journal* raised some pertinent practical and ethical questions. If a company remains constantly vulnerable to raids by corporate pirates, how will its managers be free to sacrifice short term profits to make long term investments they believe are in the best interests of the company and the community? Is blackmail of any kind ever permissible? How can raiders like Goldsmith and those who help them justify the enormous profits they receive without having any real involvement in the community and investment in the corporation? How can you hurt so many people, and have this turn out to the benefit of any one, even the corporate raider? At the confrontation in Washington, congressman John Seiberling put it forcefully: "Mr. Goldsmith...my question is, 'Who the hell are you?'" This represented the social ethic of midwestern America challenging the amorality of the international financial jet set.

Financing the War: Junkbondsmanship

The dynamo for it all is the ability to raise fabulous sums of

money quickly and easily. It is common with investment
bankers to point to the abundance of cash available to those
who know how to get it. Michael Thomas attributes this to the
financial glut created by the collapse of the commodity market
and the wage inflation of the 70s. The anticipated increase in
the price of copper, oil, farmland, and labor did not material-
ize, and so the extra money printed to handle the inflation
became the reservoir for money managers.

More exactly, the primary tactic for cornering these re-
serves of cash is what Forbes magazine (Aug. 25, '86, 34f.) calls
"the junk takeover phenomenon." The junk bond has long
been considered unsalable to the traditionally conservative
banking world. It is issued by corporations more deeply in debt
than has been considered safe, offering an interest rate that
often runs two or more percentage points higher than conven-
tional bonds. These can be purchased cheaply and in large
quantity and have become the principal means of financing the
take-over war. A Salomon Brothers, Inc. study estimates that
of the $69.5 billion in junk bonds issued since 1981, two-thirds
to three-fourths have been used to finance mergers and takeovers. (*The Wall Street Journal,* Dec. 3, '86, 16)

Playing On the Edge

The principal figure in this phenomenon has been Mike
Milken whom *Forbes,* in a flight of hyperbole, called "the leading financier of our time." An employee of Drexel, Burnham
and Lambert, and not then a corporate officer, he almost
single-handedly turned this investment banking firm into what
Business Week has called the pre-eminent financier of hostile
takeovers. Milken seized upon a way to exploit an anomaly in
the capital market by buying cheap equity with the proceeds
from bonds which previously no one wanted, but which now
under his magical ministrations had become respectable.
Forbes' source estimates that Milken's department produced
$225 million of Drexel's $350 million profit in 1985, yielding

him about $35 million in salary and bonuses. As a result of this and other stock and holdings, his personal fortune has been estimated at around "half a billion and rising." Not bad for a young man in his early forties who was head cheerleader of Birmingham High School in Van Nuys, California.

Milken lives modestly in Encino with his wife and children and insists that what he wants to do is help restore American business to owner-management so as to enable tired old public corporations to compete effectively with the Japanese. Possessed of enormous drive and ambition, as one acquaintance put it, "Michael wants to win the game...to have it all." According to these descriptions, beyond wealth would seem to be an inordinate desire for power.

Ethically, he raises several questions which involve the whole concept of junk bond financing. They also involve his own personal style of living and dealing on the edge of legality and morality where the distinctions are very hard to make. Is he hero or villain? One gets varying estimates. The SEC opted for the latter and has been raising many questions of illegality, putting both Milken and Drexel under the same kind of intense scrutiny which U.S. Attorney Rudolph W. Giuliani used so successfully against the Mafia in New York. The legal questions deal with such matters as possible conspiracy in the rigging of takeover deals, possible insider trading, disseminating confidential information to a secret network of customers, coercion, and helping clients conceal ownership of large blocks of stock. Research by *Business Week* magazine (Aug. 10, '87, 59) pointed to many sources who believed that the government would find enough grounds to bring a case against Drexel, Milken, other Drexel executives and some of their raider clients.

Since then, DBL has been charged by the government with unethical conduct and, according to the MacNeil-Lehrer Report (6/9/88) has been spending $150 million on advertising and contributions to senators to re-furbish their image. On Sept. 7, both DBL and Milken were indicted for insider trading and other illegal stock manipulation practices. (CBS News,

9/7/88) In April, 1989, a federal grand jury charged Milken, his brother Lowell and Bruce Lee Newberg, a former colleague at DBL, with a total of 98 felony counts of stock manipulation, insider trading, racketeering and other crimes. The indictment claims the forfeiture of their total $1.5 billion compensation for 1984 through 1987, and fines of $3.7 billion. If they are convicted, Milken himself could receive a maximum sentence of 520 years. (*Time, 4/10/89*) All of this signals the waning, if not the end, of Milken's junk bond network and the decline of Drexel's market share of U.S. corporate underwritings, which dropped in the first half of 1987 from 12.5 per cent to 7.3 per cent. According to *Business Week*, because of the publicity about the government investigation, along with the heightened competition spurred by Drexel's troubles, this leader in junk bond financing has not arranged financing for a single major hostile takeover since the Boesky scandal broke (see below). It would seem fairly clear that at certain points Milken and Drexel have pushed their operation beyond the edge of legality and the SEC and public opinion are catching up with them.

Legal Is Not Necessarily Ethical

But that cannot be the end of the story, for mere legality does not describe the extent of the problem. Many things are legal, but they are far from ethical in the light of any ethic worth its salt. The major ethical question has to do with debt financing itself, the heart of the junk bond industry, and the financial fuel for Drexel's gigantic takeover operation. As *Forbes* puts it, "Thanks to Milken, it's respectable for corporations to carry staggering amounts of debt...indeed, it's dangerous not to, lest one of the raiders Milken bankrolls takes you over."

The loss of financial value is a clear indication of financial inadequacy; but a more searching question is how do you define "excessive risk" in terms of ethical strategy? Making a profit is not always a good indication of economic health. One could very well make some money on a perfectly legal tactic that is actually immoral and ultimately disastrous and we need to be able to determine this before the disaster occurs. That becomes not just a problem of tactical expediency, but a question of ethics and long range strategy. We need to know ahead of time what is the right thing to do in the confidence that what is right or just is that which will work the best for both present and future. We are fairly good at predicting the economic future in terms of the so-called laws of economics, although the wide difference in the opinions of experts suggests this is far from an exact science. But we are not good at all in predicting the future in terms of the ethical laws of the universe. Here is where the Greed Syndrome finds its climate for operation.

By now, several Judeo-Christian tests have become evident in this study which can be applied to this question. Does the use of high risk junk bonds make money for an individual or corporation by jeopardizing the interests of others? Or is it a way of mortgaging the long-term future of a corporation, or an economy, for the immediate short-term benefit of a few? Is it therefore a responsible method of finance, or does it threaten the orderly structure of society where the freedom to do such things must be balanced by restraint and laws against the abuse of that freedom, where the benefit to an individual or small group must be balanced against the welfare of the whole? In other words, is it a just process? Seen in this light, it would seem that this whole game of hot air financing, played on the edge of legality, is morally bankrupt. Excessive risk represents an acceptable level of uncertainty become pathological. As such, it is an expression of the Greed Syndrome because it is out of tune with the justice of God. This means that, ultimately, it won't work. It is financially wrong because it is ethically wrong. And it is interesting to see the recent decline in revenue on the part of some of the investment banking houses dealing extensively in junk bonds, some of which have begun to show a new conservatism in junk bond trading.

Risk Arbitraging: Profiteering on the War

In any war there are always those who operate on the fringe of the battle ready to seize upon the opportunities for huge profit which such a situation affords. Such would seem to be the role of the risk arbitrageurs whose recent operations are just now becoming generally understood. The phenomenon of arbitrage has been around for a long time. For example, the practice of buying and selling national currencies in expectation of the rise and fall of the money market. This is an accepted practice and not under investigation at this time. But "risk arbitrage" is. And there would seem to be an important difference. This has become one of the principal by-products of the merger-mania described above. When a merger is threatened, a discrepancy develops between the cash value of the company and the price of its stock on the Wall Street market. The discrepancy comes because the deal may not go through, in which case the stock price will not rise to the anticipated height. The arbitrageur gives a price above the current market value of the stock anticipating that, with the merger, the price will go higher. So he buys from those who do not want to take the risk of waiting until the merger is consummated. The excessive nature of this risk is what seems to make the difference between this and other types of arbitrage. This practice has been fueled by the escalation of mergers in recent years from $12 billion in 1971 to $144 billion in 1985. The difference seems to be the line between a valid profit motive and the Greed Syndrome. As one economist put it recently, a major cause of the stock market crash of October 19, 1987, was the gambler mentality that has prevailed along Wall Street in recent years.

Ivan The Terrible

More recently, this whole situation has been under investigation by the SEC, and especially the activities of a particular network of arbitrageurs revolving around Ivan Boesky. His case has become a classic illustration of the possibilities and problems of this type of high finance. After an undistinguished academic and business beginning, Boesky acquired a degree from the Detroit College of Law, married the daughter of a wealthy real-estate developer, and with her family funds started his own arbitrage firm in 1975. Working very hard, he quickly became known for his aggressive trading of stocks in multi-million dollar lots and for his skill in high risk arbitrage. In 1977, he made his first big score, receiving $7 million in the takeover of Babcock & Wilcox. Following that, his fortunes waxed and waned, losing $20 million on Cities Service stock when Gulf failed to take it over and $70 million when T. Boone Pickens was unable to take over Phillips Petroleum, but netting $65 million when Chevron took over Gulf. His downfall came in 1985 when he was caught using illegal insider trading information which he obtained from Dennis Levine, an employee of Drexel, Burnham & Lambert, to make what the SEC determined was profits of at least $50 million from takeover and corporate restructuring deals. (*Newsweek*, Dec. 1, '86) The callous self-interest within this process is characterized by Boesky in a now famous one-liner: "It may seem callous, but I am indifferent to who succeeds or fails as long as I make a profit."

At this point, the SEC went into action. Gary Lynch, its Director of Enforcement, along with a staff of 600, set about unravelling what has been called the largest insider trading scandal in Wall Street history. Shock waves went up and down the Street as Levine, Boesky and several others were arrested. Drexel, along with a host of individuals and investment banking houses was brought under investigation. Boesky made a deal with the SEC to inform on those with whom he had been trading on insider information, even to taping their private conversations, thus insuring him of no more than five years in jail. In what appears as a hollow confession, Boesky said in a statement released after his arrest by the SEC, "If my mistakes launch a process of re-examination of the rules and practices of our financial market-place, then perhaps some good will result."

The Mentality of Dishonesty

The most obvious problem with this is that much that is going on is against the law, and, like Boesky and Levine, you might get caught. The history of the last few years is replete with illustrations of stealing, fraud, stock-churning, money-laundering, misuse of discretionary accounts, inside information, shrouding the investigation of investor complaints in secrecy, with brokers chairing the hearings, and with judgments almost impossible to appeal. *Newsweek* (Dec. 22, '86, 42f.) has done a service in its investigative reporting of this crisis of trust within the investment community. It would seem that the small investor more and more is becoming convinced that the deck is stacked against him. It isn't just Boesky and the arbitrageurs, but rather a widespread attitude and set of tactics that have infiltrated large segments of the investment banking industry. How widespread this is will be a matter of considerable investigation. Jay L. Walker has produced a book entitled *The Complete Book of Wall Street Ethics*. Except for one quote by Ivan Boesky, the pages are all blank.

There are, of course, many illustrations of honesty and integrity on Wall Street, and probably more concern for these matters there than anywhere else; but there would seem to be an abundance of fuel behind this fire. According to Friday and Pauly in their study, thousands of investors have been filing complaints with the SEC: in 1986, these totaled 15,915, up 128 per cent in just four years. It would seem that the Greed Syndrome is operating with special virulence within this investment banking sector, symptomized most visibly by the excess of dishonesty which has surfaced within it. Dishonesty is always the pus that identifies a point of moral infection. Getting so close to so much money would be an almost overwhelming temptation to anyone. *Business Week* (Dec. 1, '86, 29) quotes

New York securities lawyer Meredith M. Brown commenting on this situation: "There will be hearings, and everyone will be amazed at the extent of human greed."

But the mentality of dishonesty we are witnessing is more than just a clever concern to avoid the law. It has a more subtle and distinctive quality. It is, for example, part of our ethical throwaway culture where honesty is dispensable and dishonesty becomes justified because it is efficient, or a matter of survival, or of making a killing in the stock market. As Thomas put it, "The new breed are utterly confident. In the face of such driving certitude, honesty is merely another variable in their splendid ethically neutral calculus of personal profit." There is something sick about such a culture.

The dishonesty we are talking about is not only illegal, but more often para-legal, where men and women are operating on the edge of legality where there is no distinction made between what is illegal and what is unethical. Donald Shriver, President of Union Seminary in New York, put it succinctly: "Dishonesty is wrong even if it is legal." Ivan Boesky has done us more of a service than his shallow grasp of the ethical process allows him to realize. In his naive amorality he has given us a classic expression of the current mentality of dishonesty in his inability to distinguish between greed and the profit motive. At a business school graduation, in a statement greeted with laughter and applause, he is quoted as saying, "Greed is all right...I want you to know that I think greed is healthy. You can be greedy and still feel good about yourself." He spells out this philosophy at length in his book, *Merger Mania, Arbitrage: Wall Street's Best Kept Secret*. Like the happy hooker, this Wall Street buccaneer seems blithely unaware of the moral disease germs he has been spreading.

An emerging thesis of these pages is that greed is an acceptable and necessary profit motive out of control. Like a cancer, it is a normal part of economic life become pathological and so, destructive.

The deeper character flaw behind the current face of dishonesty is that the Boeskys of this nation have not been able to go beyond the legal to the ethical dimensions of the problem. A clear ethical justification must always underlie any law if it is to be obeyed. As NAM's Gault put it in testifying before a House Energy and Commerce Subcommittee, "The recent spate of indictments exposing the greed and amoral attitude of some Wall Street players is an indictment of a system in trouble." Apparently, a large segment of our nation is not convinced of the necessity for honesty. The popular mind would say that Boesky's problem was not ethical, but merely legal. He did the inexcusable. He got caught.

So why not be dishonest if the odds are that we won't get caught? The high risk nature of modern finance is really an expression of the current gambling mentality. We get used to playing the odds. We need more than just fear of exposure to curb this wave. We need a clearly defined ethic that goes beyond the law to some absolute that is right because it is right because it is right. Our age has given up such archaic things...almost. For there is a cloying recollection of something we learned as children to the effect that "Thou shalt not steal." Despite our current atheism, we have a feeling that there just might be something to this.

For the ancient Hebrew prophet, this commandment was an affirmation of the sanctity of life. Property is really an extension of ourselves, a source of happiness and an essential for survival. This commandment restrains offenses against persons. It also is an expression of God's justice and a reminder that stealing in any form destroys an economy. Dishonesty violates not only the rights of those who have property, but also the rights of all men and women to be able to own property. This is our birthright. This kind of amoral, para-legal, ethically naive moral calculus robs us of that birthright. There is a clear formula here which strikes to the heart of our problem. Stealing is a form of atheism, a rejection of the justice of God which leads inevitably to the downward spiral of God's judgment: frustration, cynicism, dishonesty, some form of violence and ultimately destruction. It just doesn't work.

Black Monday and the Question of Value

The calamity of "Black Monday" on Wall Street, occurring on the very day these words were written, although not, I am sure, timed to coincide with the outline of this chapter, does, indeed, raise exactly the ethical-financial question that needs to be posed at this point. Is the loose-lipped, amoral, flamboyant, casino warfare situation on Wall Street, and the merger mania sweeping the country, good for the economy?

A growing chorus of voices is saying that our economy is too vulnerable to withstand these extremities of risk-taking. What has been emerging in this study is a situation where the making of large sums of money has become an end in itself, a game, a way of making points. The stock market has been moving, perhaps more truly than ever before, from a business situation, where risk is nominal and under control, to a gambling enterprise, where the risks are beyond the bounds of prudence and out of our control, and where the deck is often stacked against us. As we have already pointed out, this gambling mentality is a form of prostitution where a pleasurable activity, like making money, becomes an end in itself dedicated to short term pleasure, begetting nothing, creating all kinds of problems, tending to escalate, and leading to disease and death.

Pat Choate, economist for TRW Inc., warns in *Business Week* (Nov. 24, '86) that "the big wave of takeovers is creating an unstable situation for the economy." It's all a very large gamble and if it doesn't pay off, it could stop corporate restructuring cold. "Too much leveraging...too much gambling mentality on Wall Street": these diagnoses of the crash of 1987 by a leading economist and the chairman of the New York Stock Exchange would seem to bear out Choate's prophetic warning. And nothing has really changed. A year after the Wall Street crash, one analyst in an NBC report (10/18/88) insisted "the seeds of destruction are still in place." Problem: too much speculation and risk-taking.

At issue is what Adam Smith reminded us of years ago: the

wealth of nations is a question of value. In order to survive, the economy of a nation must be based on the creation of genuine value whether one locates this, as Smith did, in the labor expended, or in natural resources, in one's industrial might or in the more current basis of communication and services. What seems to be developing in our nation is a gambler's standard of value based upon who happens to have the most cash. Roger Smith, GM chairman, warned recently that the Wall Street speculators and corporate raiders were undermining trust in the financial system. Business, he said, "is more than a money game. It's the art of producing quality goods and services." This is a warning that has become increasingly insistent in most of the business and economic journals of the day. Now since Black Monday it has radically increased in volume.

The problem with the current scene, whether we are talking about the takeover war or the misuse of the stock market, is that we have not been producing anything of value. We have merely been moving the money and property around like the pieces on a monopoly board and, in the process destroying much that has been the source of all that wealth. It is as if a bunch of cool-headed, cold-hearted, highly competitive, prodigiously aggressive and excessively greedy men (there are few women) sit in a sound-proofed back room playing a gigantic high-stakes game of Monopoly with our money. Their only concern is to see who can amass the largest pile without any concern for the effect on the economy, the stability of the nation, the jobs lost, the careers destroyed, the communities blasted by their moving companies around like lifeless pieces on the board. They create no value and only benefit themselves and a limited number of cronies who latch on to them in order to make their own pile of money. We seem to be at the mercy of immoral, or at best, amoral men. This is a potentially disastrous situation where one kind of greed begets another, until all kinds of greed operate together to form the syndrome that, like a cancer, destroys some part of the social structure. *Time* magazine's indictment that these financial crooks "are only paper shufflers and money changers" would seem to be in order. (May 25, '87, 22)

Our tests of value in recent months seem to have been those of efficiency, cash flow and size of bank account or the power of our corporate structure without worrying too much about the ethics of what we have been doing. As Day-Lower put this logic of profitless profit, "Managers of capital may cease making much of anything at all except more capital, by turning their attention from production to acquisitions, mergers and money market manipulations. Profits improve, but the capacity to produce becomes obsolete." It would seem that we must distinguish between profit and value and learn again an old lesson that it is value, not profit, which is the source of the wealth of nations.

Justice and the Current Financial Climate

Short-range over long-range benefit to a few at the expense of the many, profit over persons, coercion and the denial of freedom in the market place, efficiency over social welfare, too much permissiveness within the economy, too little restraint and the enforcement of laws already on the books, that is, too little concern for the ethical laws of God's justice, have begotten a situation within the economy for which the market collapse of October, 1987, was a foregone ethical conclusion. God's judgment is constantly at work within the investment banking community as it is within all aspects of life. James Gleich, in *The New York Times* (Nov. 22, '87), described what had been happening on Wall Street as economic chaos. Whatever else it may have been in terms of economic theory, political strategy or financial tactics, and we will be debating these matters for years, it would seem clear that this has been a particularly dramatic illustration of *ethical* chaos, of the interdependence and vulnerability of our economy, and the ethical bankruptcy that provides the climate for the Greed Syndrome.

Chapter 7

Someone Else Must Pay for My Trouble

"Americans have the greatest proclivity to sue of any nation on earth." Ohio Appellate Judge John R. Milligan thus summarizes what Tom Moyer, the Chief Justice of the Ohio Supreme Court, calls "Hyperlexia," the overwhelming escalation of litigation in recent years throughout America. *Forbes* magazine reports that from 1974 to 1985 product liability actions in federal courts alone increased by 758 per cent. In 1984 it was estimated that the liability law system cost 37 times what it did in 1950. Some responsible sources predicted that in 1988 one out of 12 to 15 Americans would be involved in a lawsuit. In that year, The National Association of Manufacturers identified product liability litigation as one of the major causes of trouble in U.S. industry. As former Chief Justice Burger put it, our society today "has an almost irrational focus — virtually a mania — on litigation as the way to solve problems."

The driving energy behind all this would seem to be an extension of the Greed Syndrome producing a litigation crisis of major proportions in many areas, but especially those of tort law, insurance and medicine. Greed has many faces and many extenuations as it spreads its poison into these aspects of the American scene.

A Bizarre Rash of Symptoms

In recent months, we have been inundated by reports of law suits seeming to come from a fantasy world where expectations are unheard of and the rewards are unbelievable. As one judge put it, the best bet today for making a fast buck is not the lottery, but suing. The odds of your making a large amount of money through litigation are very high. So why not join the rush to court?

It is often pointed out by those in industry that it is practically impossible to manufacture, distribute or sell a product today that won't end up in court somewhere. Out of the 13 million private civil law suits filed in state and federal courts last year some stand out with peculiar clarity and will probably go down in American folklore as illustrations of a strange mania that seized Americans in the 1980s.

Item: An overweight man with a history of heart disease had a heart attack while starting a Sears lawn mower. He sued Sears, charging that the pull rope required too much effort. A Pennsylvania jury awarded him $1.2 million, along with $550,000 in punitive damages because Sears did not settle the claim promptly.

Item: An oft-reported case is that of an 18 year old burglar who fell through a painted-over skylight while stealing lights from the roof of a public school in Redding, California. Paralyzed by the fall, he sued the school district and recovered $260,000, plus $1500 a month for life in an out-of-court settlement.

Item: A car full of beer-drinking teen-agers careened at 60 mph, twice the posted speed limit, down a street in Antioch, California. It smashed into a light pole and one passenger died, with two others badly injured. The driver was convicted of manslaughter. Lawyers for the passengers, however, sued everybody they could find: Antioch, a nearby shopping center, even the utility company that owned the light pole. They settled the case out of court for $850,000.

Item: An eight year old ran out into the street and into the side of a GM car. The side view mirror hit the child causing severe brain damage. The child, who had been left in the care of a thirteen year old, sued his parents for failure to provide adequate supervision and was awarded $100,000. The driver was sued for failure to maintain an adequate lookout. The jury awarded the plaintiff $100,000. The parents then sued General Motors for $6 million for creating a non-crashworthy mirror. The case is still pending.

Then there is the case of the Stanley screwdriver. A man used one of these to open a paint can. The end of the can flipped off and put out his eye. Since the man was in an occupation in which he badly needed his eyes, he sued Stanley for $6 million. He won the suit on the grounds that the manufacturer had failed to warn him of this danger.

The epidemic of litigation is not limited to product liability. The *Cleveland Plain Dealer* (Dec. 3, '87) reports that when Cory Snyder was at bat, he swung and missed. The bat slipped and struck two women in the stands. They promptly sued him for $2 million, but the case was lost because of the disclaimer on the back of the ticket. Even ten years ago, such a suit would probably never have been filed.

In the previous 18 months *Church Management*, a clergy journal, reported that $100 million in lawsuits had been initiated against pastors and churches for a variety of causes, leading many to take out liability insurance. Times have changed, and one wonders what is happening to our nation as reflected in our courts.

The pattern running throughout these and a plethora of similar cases is their bizarre character, the common sense question as to the justice of the case, and the suggestion of greed as a primary motivation. One clear trend is that which is observed by many in the court system: there seems to be a clear drift toward awarding the plaintiff, no matter what the circumstances. The other major trend is the dramatic escalation of the number of such suits and the size of the awards.

How Deep Is the Pocket?

One of the most dramatic and far-reaching types of cases is that involving what is called "joint and several liability." If two parties have some degree of responsibility for an injury and one cannot pay, then the one who can must pay the entire damage award, no matter how small be the responsibility. This is sometimes called "the deep pocket principle" because the party with the deepest pocket must always pay, whatever the fault.

A case in point comes from north central Ohio. The Will Burt Co., in Orrville, manufactured metal parts for a multitude of different firms and purposes. One of these was The Hi-Lo Powered Scaffolding Co. in Cincinnati for which Will Burt manufactured about 50 per cent of the parts. In 1980, two men working for a Florida company were using a scaffold made by Hi-Lo in 1966. The scaffolding failed and the men fell, one to his death and the other badly hurt. The defense argued that the 16 year old ladder had been poorly maintained and the men were using it improperly, ignoring the warnings affixed to it. The family sued the company for $6 million. Hi-Lo promptly declared bankruptcy. You can't collect from a bankrupt company.

The plaintiff's lawyers then began a process of what is called "shotgunning," shooting at everyone who had had the slightest connection with the product, whether they made a screw or a motor or the metal that went into the ladder. The Cincinnati ladder company had gone out of business, so there was nothing there. Down the line was Will Burt, and the courts ruled that since it had made some of the parts and since it had an insurance policy, according to what is called "strict liability" it was responsible and must pay the entire amount. This Will Burt's insurance company did, but in August 1985, Will Burt received a call that its insurance had been cancelled. Unable to find other insurance, it was forced out of business.

But that was not the end of the story. Harry Featherstone, president of the company, is a fighter. He began an intensive and extended battle in court and in appeals to State and Federal legislatures to change the laws which permit what he considered to be a completely unjust situation. In one reported teleconference with a federal judge and a professor at Chicago University, the judge, in answer to Featherstone's objection, said, "Harry, if I have a victim in my court and an innocent defendant, the defendant will always lose to the victim. When somebody is hurt, somebody has to pay, and that's the way my court believes." When Featherstone challenged the fairness of such a policy, the judge replied, "I don't know how to answer you," and terminated the teleconference.

With the common sense peculiar to residents of small midwestern towns, this industrialist-turned-reformer had challenged the professors and administrators of American law with a profound ethical question. They could give him no answer. But this is one of the most relevant questions facing the legal system today. Beyond what individual judges or juries or lawyers do or say in the litigation of particular cases, the American people want to know what has happened to justice in the courts of the land.

The Litigation Crisis

We seem to be in some kind of crisis situation with every state in the Union considering legislation to correct some of the most extreme anomalies. In attempting to analyze the situation, the escalation of litigation would appear to revolve around three main professions: the law, insurance and medicine. The most basic question is what do we mean by justice? The principal questions for jurisprudence have to do with fault and responsibility. The medical problem seems to revolve around the avoidance of suffering and the search for health. The issues involving the insurance industry focus on risk and safety. For the sake of clarity, each of these areas will be considered separately, although they are all part of the same general set of problems.

We're Living in a Different World

The reasons given for the escalation of litigation in this generation run the gamut of social change which has been going on for a long time and has come to dramatic focus in the last decade. Clearly, the Greed Syndrome is operating in the courts just as surely as it is on Wall Street. In the words of Prof. Ralph L. Barnett, chairman of Triodyne Inc., a firm that has investigated about 10,000 liability cases for both defendants and plaintiffs in recent years, "A product liability lawsuit starts with greed in a court climate that favors the plaintiff and his (or her) attorneys."

The technological changes occurring within this generation are well documented; progress has been phenomenal, with new products, new services, new techniques, each one raising questions about safety, morality and justice. What is being more and more recognized by the courts is that, as one judge put it, technology has been running ahead of our understanding of what is moral and what is right. We are living in a much more complex world and are expecting the courts to catch us up on a generation of ethical inattention. But we are finding that they, like the rest of us, are ill-equipped to do so.

We have discussed the quality and extent of our national affluence and some of the fallout in society. What the courts are facing is a situation in which fabulous sums of money are available and where there are many "deep pockets." Coupled with the prevailing drive toward becoming rich as quickly and easily as possible, it is no wonder there is a firestorm of greed erupting within the courts. The legal route is the quickest, easiest and surest way to make a fortune in America today. Just sue somebody. There is a rush toward legislative defense against abuse: this should help; but as long as hedonism remains the dominant American attitude, the courts will continue to be vulnerable as we get more and more skillful in manipulating the law.

The prevailing climate of individualism in America manifests itself in the tremendous drive to get rich, to succeed, to be number one, to find the good life. Sometimes it is called "the American way." In the legal area, this comes out in the determination of individuals to take the law into their own hands through litigation, to express their anger, frustration, sense of injustice, desire for vengeance, or just plain greed through the power that enables them to bring the most powerful agencies in the land, even the government, to account. This is a precious inheritance and one we would all defend. But this American right is being abused. In the process our freedom is being eroded. With every great blessing goes an equally great responsibility, but it is our responsibility within the law that is being brought into question.

The American Dream itself has been going through a series of changes, as our affluence and technology convince us of the unlimited possibilities in this abundant land. But we have over-sold this concept to the point that our expectations are exaggerated and completely unrealistic. The American Dream has become a strange kind of nightmare, fueled by our drive for what Prof. Lawrence Friedman of Stanford in his book, *Total Justice*, has called "a higher level of justice" and what others might call an escalation of self-interest. We literally expect that science, technology and the courts are capable of solving all our problems. We are impatient when they don't. This manifests itself in the widespread attitude that we have a right to expect a trouble-free life. The strangeness of some of the suits, judgments and settlements in the courts in recent years would appear to be the working out of the logic of this unreal fantasy world which is really a prostitution of the American dream. In that kind of world, it is completely logical to say that "somebody else must pay for my trouble."

The New Climate in the Courts

The social battle of the 1960s was fought out on the streets, in the colleges and in the courts. It produced many profound changes, some of them good, some bad, but all to be reckoned with. The courts in recent years have clearly reflected the influence of that social movement which favored the poor over the rich, the weak over the strong, the victim over the victimizer, the deviant over the normal. The propensity of judges and juries to reward the plaintiff, no matter what the suit, to soak the rich, the insurance companies and the government, no matter what the cost or the result, would seem to be a clear extension of that series of attitudes characterizing the social civil war of the 1960s. We were left with a profound distrust of the search for justice either in the government or in the courts. That distrust produced a widespread concern to take matters legally into our own hands and make the legal process serve the cause of social change.

Richard Willard, chief of the Justice Department's civil division, charges that some judges and lawyers are using the courts "to restructure society and administer a massive scheme for the redistribution of wealth." Whether good or bad, this is legislation through litigation and represents an important development in the concept of the separation of powers.

The trend has resulted in the radical liberalizing of tort law, that aspect of the law dealing with liability, and, as Canton's Appellate Judge Milligan expressed it, has served to open the floodgate of litigation and greed. Now the rights of recovery have been extended in so many different directions it is possible to sue nearly anybody for almost anything. The concept of strict liability, for example, enables the claimants to recover damages for injuries caused by manufactured products without regard to fault or direct connection with an injury. This is the basis of the "deep pocket" principle involved in the Will Burt case: payment should come not from the one who is at fault, but from the one who can pay.

A decade ago, injured persons whose own carelessness was responsible for injury could not often successfully prosecute. Since the mid-1970s, however, ten states have adopted comparative fault standards which allow plaintiffs to recover damages even if they share the fault with the manufacturer. *U.S. News and World Report* cites several cases to illustrate this point. (Jan. 27, '86, 35f.) A New Jersey court said merchants could be held liable if a customer's dog bit another patron. A Maryland court held that handgun makers could be forced to pay damages resulting from a shooting. A California policeman agreed to pay damages when a woman who bought his house complained he hadn't disclosed five murders committed there 12 years earlier. Employees injured on the job can now not only collect workers compensation, but often sue the makers of the equipment involved in an accident.

In the operation of the Greed Syndrome, there is no limit to the creative ingenuity of lawyers and plaintiffs in dreaming up new kinds of tort liability. An ABA committee in 1985 praised what it called "the resilience" of the law in responding to social change, a development credited in part to "imaginative lawyering." This kind of support has encouraged an epidemic of what many are calling frivolous suits. There is, for example, the classic case of the California tree trimmer who charged in a suit that eating Hostess cupcakes and similar products had given him "toxic-junk syndrome." A Pennsylvania mother's baby choked on peanut butter. She sued the makers, charging that they should have warned customers of the danger to infants. Most of such suits are thrown out of court, but they illustrate the phenomenon we are describing. We have become a "sue-happy" society.

The question is not the laudable concern to protect the weak and innocent and raise the condition of the downtrodden; laws must be responsive to changing times and the needs of all persons, especially those who cannot defend themselves. The problem seems to be that the laws have become prostituted by the excesses of greed. We are facing a blaze of litigation fanned, if not sparked, by greed. The shining vistas of Kennedy's idealized Camelot have become tarnished by the ethical bankruptcy of a nation that has been more interested in the adultery of Lancelot than in the ideals of King Arthur.

Who Is the Aggressor?

The suggestion coming from the evidence so far is that the driving force for the abuse of the legal system comes from greedy plaintiffs, average citizens caught up in the hedonism of this affluent society with its radical disparity between the rich and the poor. Another candidate, who has become so identified with the problem as to be almost synonymous with it, is the legal profession. We are being reminded these days that there are more lawyers per capita in America than in any nation on earth. *U.S. News and World Report* (Jan. 27, '86) records that in 1986 there were 700,000 lawyers in this country, one for every 350 Americans, collecting $55 billion a year in fees. This is three times as many as in England and more than 20 times as many as in Japan. John Naisbitt, in his book *Megatrends,* points out that this number has increased from 250,000 in 1960. In the opinion of the ABA, it will increase to over a million by the mid-1990s. According to the 1983 report of the U.S. Bureau of Labor Statistics, the paralegal profession has been growing even faster. If we are indeed the most litigious nation on earth, this professional stampede would seem to be clear evidence.

The problem is that this burgeoning supply of lawyers and paralegals is only partially the result of an expanded need. There is much money to be made and there is evidence that the Greed Syndrome is operating with particular virulence within this profession. The last census lists the average lawyer's salary as $43,900. Since then the situation has escalated and it is anybody's guess how much lawyers are making. In 1984, *Fortune* magazine (Nov. 26, 181f.) estimated that the top partners in Milberg Weiss, America's largest law firm specializing in shareholder litigation, made in excess of $400,000 a year. With the increase of liability litigation in more recent years, the escalation of awards into the millions, and the prevalence of contingency fees averaging between 20 and 50 per cent, the figure is no doubt considerably higher. The Chamber of Commerce cites statistics that the average product liability award has increased from $345,000 to more than $1 million in the last ten years. In asbestos litigation, of the average $101,000 award or settlement, lawyers received $62,000. (Jan Greene, *American Market Metal Working News*, Dec. 16, '85) As one lawyer is recently reported saying: "Product liability is lucrative business and we are going to stay with it as long as we can."

Another aspect of what would seem to be the operation of the Greed Syndrome has to do with a whole series of less visible, but equally lucrative practices within the ordinary conduct of the law. Critics charge that some lawyers operating on an hourly fee are provoking or prolonging litigation unnecessarily in order to maintain their income level in the face of increasing competition. The many kinds of motions that delay a trial, extra costs for discovery, hiring unnecessary experts, excessive trial preparation, appeals, settling only at the last minute on the steps of the courthouse, all are ways of increasing the cost of litigation. Roger Fisher, an expert in negotiation and the settlement of disputes, points in *The Harvard Business Review* (March-April, '85, 63, 15-19) to the conflicts of interest that create a dis-incentive for lawyers to prosecute a case speedily and efficiently. "A big case is to a law firm as a good milking cow is to a dairy farmer." Young associates in some firms are expected to turn in a large number of billable hours. The more of these they turn in, the better their chances for making partner. The Product Liability Alliance, a coalition of trade associations, manufacturers, sellers and insurers, charges that lawyers receive more than claimants in typical product liability cases and this "gives the plaintiff's attorneys a vested interest in maintaining the current chaotic state of affairs." (*Fact Sheet*, Dec. '85)

Time Magazine in a recent study of America's largest law firms (Dec. 7, '87, 58f.) documents the growth of the business mentality within this profession. High starting salaries, preference for what are called "rainmakers," the partners most adept at bringing in clients, the growth of hourly rates to as much as $350 an hour, the expectation that, in order to earn their keep, associates must rack up at least 2,000 billable hours annually, all describe the scenario for the phenomenal growth in costs. The competition for this money bonanza has fueled a merger boom among firms and prompted what *Time* called "A boom in ethical lapses that includes such things as the bribing of witnesses, insider trading and getting too close to the action in handling corporate mergers."

All of this is causing the legal profession considerable anxiety with what former Chief Justice Warren Burger called "the widespread hue and cry about lawyers' fees and litigation costs." As a result, under the revision of the rules of federal civil procedure, approved by the Supreme Court in 1983, judges are required to do something whenever they encounter attorneys using these fee-hyping tactics. In 1984 a special committee within the ABA released the results of a five year study, declaring: "the high cost of litigation is a matter of critical concern. It is ethically wrong for the judicial resolution of disputes to be prohibitively expensive."

Product Liability Is the Focus

Product liability suits seem to be a special arena for this legal game. Ralph Barnett, whose firm handles about three percent of all mechanical engineering lawsuits in the U.S., observes that in his experience, "product liability becomes a no-win situation. Leave a hazard unshielded and the plaintiff will argue a shield should have been installed. If a guard is removed by a user, the plaintiff will argue the guard should have been hinged. If it was hinged, the plaintiff, or his attorneys, will argue there should have been an interlock to prevent machine operation with the guard out of place. Install an interlock and they will argue for a double interlock, or a failsafe system to protect the worker from himself."

The leader in the campaign for expanded liability concepts is the Association of Trial Lawyers of America, a Washington-based organization of some 60,000 attorneys for plaintiffs. This group, in the words of its president, Robert L. Habush, is committed "to strengthening the civil justice system as an instrument to make victims whole and society safer." This is a noble end; but, whether fairly or not, its vigorous defense of the contingency fee and its opposition to most legislative attempts to curb the enormous financial benefits from the excess of litigation have gained this organization the reputation for being the driving energy behind the growth of the Greed Syndrome within the plaintiff's bar. The magazine, *Trial*, the official organ of this association, promotes that impression with its emphasis on how to increase the size of profits from litigation. One ad by The Legal Marketing Group is typical: "61 million personal injuries will occur this year. If your firm wants a substantial increase in new cases, call The Legal Marketing Group, the leader in syndicated and customized legal advertising. We will send you a sample of our pre-tested, award-winning commercials." This seems to be a major source of the emergence into semi-respectability of what used to be called "ambulance chasing." We are all familiar with the current rash of TV advertising, and the constant offer to help us sue somebody for something.

Concern for the dignity of the legal profession is growing within the ATLA, although there is some disagreement as to priorities. Robert Habush writes in *Trial* (Nov. '86, 5) that the insurance crisis has somewhat changed their priorities: "We've come to realize that it's not enough to be good lawyers. We have a responsibility to be good citizens as well and to demonstrate to others that our commitment to principle is for the greater good of the whole...There could be no clearer expression of our acceptance of our responsibilities as citizens than the creation of The Civil Justice Foundation." This is high sounding rhetoric; but in its official statement in *Trial*, the foundation describes its mission "as an organization dedicated *solely* to strengthening the ties among organizations which represent consumers." (italics mine) Apparently, "the greater good of the whole" does not extend beyond the limited interests of the plaintiff's bar.

The Greed Syndrome In Operation

On a superficial level we can see some of the familiar symptoms of the Greed Syndrome operating within the legal situation. The most obvious is the prostitution of the courts to make a large amount of money as quickly and easily as possible. When money takes precedence over justice, then we are seeing the operation of the Greed Syndrome. The evidence for the profit mentality within the legal profession, the explosion of litigation, the escalation of the numbers of lawyers, the size of awards, the rash of frivolous suits are all clearly a reflection of the current hedonism and the fixation on cash as the remedy to all our problems. Whether on the part of greedy plaintiffs or unscrupulous lawyers, these are symptoms of the same individualism with its uncontrolled self-interest we have observed in other areas of our economy. When one's concern for justice is so narrowly defined that it must be achieved at the expense of others, whatever be the consequences, where cash profit takes precedence over human relationships, then we are in the presence of the Greed Syndrome.

Dishonesty is always a symptom of the virulent operation of self-interest out of control and one can see this at work in this crisis of litigation. The determination to make large quick profits with a minimum of work through legal channels raises the same problems as gambling. Although here the odds are so loaded in favor of the plaintiff that no casino or lottery would be able to operate under those conditions. The economic sterility of litigation that pushes money around without contributing anything of value to the economy partakes of the same problems as those emerging in Wall Street and the merger mania. An unfriendly suit, if unjust, poses the same ethical questions as an unfriendly takeover in business and represents a similar prostitution of the legal system. Legal piracy, concentrating on immediate cash returns without concern for the welfare of the defendant, the corporation or society in general, raises the same ethical objections as when it occurs within the corporate scene. The bizarre character of so many of the current cases, whether thrown out of court or awarded a large sum, partakes of the same unreality as the enthusiastic visions of quick and easy wealth beyond imagining which drives the corporate raiders and cruelly exploits the purchaser of the lottery ticket. The prostitution of the American dream to the acquisition of quick and extravagant wealth is typical of the operation of the Greed Syndrome, and emerges here in the fantasy world of litigation. It assumes that in America the law must provide me with a trouble-free and abundant life and this honorable profession is being exploited by everyone who is able to climb aboard the money wagon.

It's Ultimately a Question of Justice

But we are still only examining the surface of this matter. The ethical symptoms we have identified are more results than causes. Beyond the obvious matters of dishonesty and the tactics of greed, to get at what's really ethically wrong with this situation we must go more deeply into the matter of ethical strategy operating within the legal system itself. In examining the legal expression of greed, even more than in other aspects of the economy, the problem is one of justice. The Greed Syndrome operates when either the strategy or the tactics of any situation are unjust.

"When somebody is hurt, somebody has to pay." "The defendant will always lose to the victim." "It's not a matter of fault but the responsibility of the one who can afford to pay." These are some of the attitudes we have seen emerging in this study. And what's wrong with that? In some ways these legal strategies would seem to reflect the movement of our courts toward a more humane and ethical justice system where the rich are made to care for the poor, the strong are forced to be responsible for the weak. This is surely a move in the right direction. The problem is that along with some good results the current legal strategy described in this chapter would seem to be fostering the escalation of the Greed Syndrome within the exercise of American law. Along with some genuine ethical advances have gone so many problems that we are led to question the very ethical strategy of our current system. At best it is ethically immature. At worst, disastrous.

"Woe Unto You Lawyers"

Jesus was hard on lawyers. But not because there was anything intrinsically wrong with being a lawyer. Some of his larger group of disciples were Scribes and Pharisees, that is, lawyers. The great Apostle Paul was a highly trained lawyer. The problem was legalism, that is, letting the law get in the way of justice. In that famous passage in Luke (11:42-52), Jesus condemns the lawyers for paying pious attention to tithing, giving to the temple a tenth of every bit of seasoning they put in their food, but neglecting "justice and the love of God." For the Scribes and Pharisees of his day, the great prophetic tradition of justice as proclaimed by Isaiah, Jeremiah and Moses had been reduced to a massive case law system with precedents for every possible legal and ethical situation. But this fixation on the "Traditions of the Elders" (Matt.15:2), what I have called the tactics of the law, had drawn the lawyers away from the ethical strategy and basic ideology that lay behind this controversial welter of conflicting case law tactics.

"You build the tombs of the prophets." And it is the prophets who most forcefully proclaimed what Jesus reminded those lawyers. The first and greatest commandment is this, "You shall love the Lord your God with all your heart and soul and mind and strength, and your neighbor as yourself." (Mark 12:28-34) They had gotten lost in the forest of tactical legalism. Jesus tried to recall them to a renewed concern for ethical strategies and ideology, to that greatest of all revelations which described the very nature of God himself. This is what he called "the key of knowledge" (Luke 11:52), the sovereignty and justice of God: "These you ought to have done, without neglecting the others." (Matt.23:23)

The Justice Vacuum

It is a commonplace today that lawyers avoid a discussion of the justice of the various legal codes, insisting that their function is merely to apply the laws which are drafted at the legislative level. Behind this, of course, is the American system which separates the legislative from the judicial functions. This is one of the deeper problems in this inquiry into the conditions that have encouraged the Greed Syndrome. What it has done is to place the entire focus of what goes on in the courts upon the tactical administration of legal codes that may or may not have anything to do with the justice of the matter. They are litigating in a box. Within that narrow confinement of permitted evidence and required proof, of precedent and accepted procedure, have emerged decisions that are bizarre and unreal because they do not rest upon a broad enough base of justice.

The Ethics of the Separation of Powers

The radical separation of powers between the functions of the legislatures and those of the courts is promoting this situation and there is a need for an extensive review of this issue. In attempting an ethical analysis of the separation of powers between the legislative and the judicial, one must begin by recognizing that the whole area of jurisprudence is an ethical activity. It represents the political formalization of the ethical process as we decide what we should or should not do.

The doctrine of separation has been a traditional way of sorting out the problem of authority in the legal process in terms of the difference of functions. The legislatures draft the laws and the courts apply and enforce them. This makes sense since legislatures are elite groups presumably chosen for their competence and elected by the people who can throw them out if necessary. Juries, on the other hand, are popular groups chosen at random, with a minimal concern for competence in the law, and with no public recourse for recalling them. So it would seem that the drafting of our laws, our ethical strategies, should be done by the more responsible body.

The ethical problem is that one just can't separate the process of justice into functional compartments. Ideology, strategy and tactics are all involved together, at whatever functional level, whether in the legislatures or in the jury box. By the very nature of justice, legal practice, like ethical practice, is a holistic exercise. Legislatures and juries, lawyers and judges, are all involved at every moment in all three activities. They may concentrate more on drafting legal strategies or applying legal tactics because of their particular function, but inevitably they are involved in the entire ethical process. Any radical separation of function that assigns to one group exclusively the making of laws and to another simply their interpretation and application is ultimately artificial and bound to produce skewed, bizarre and unjust results. And this is exactly what we have seen happening where justice is perverted or prevented by the clever manipulation of a mass of legal technicalities. There is nothing, in this author's opinion, more damaging to public morale, respect for the courts and the prosecution of justice. When someone everyone knows is guilty is freed on a technicality, our justice system has broken down and the ethical necessity for punishment so basic to justice has been suborned. So one would have to argue that it is entirely proper, nay, indeed inevitable, that juries and courts be involved in working out new legal-ethical strategies.

Actually, the recognition of this ethical fact is coming slowly from within the system itself. Courts have recently been urged to adopt a more active role in deciding ethically strategic issues. Constitutional amendments in many states have given the courts broad rule-making authority. As a result, courts have more and more been fashioning new laws through litigation. But this is still the exception rather than the rule.

What it does is raise the problem of making juries more responsible for their decisions, often made on the basis of ignorance, prejudice, or special interest. Judges and lawyers must be more closely supervised as they argue and manipulate the law. There must be some means of restraining and regulating this process of legislation through litigation. At this point, we are into the tactical details of jurisprudence and beyond the scope or competence of this review. The ethical point is that total justice should be the primary concern at both legislative and judicial levels. Jesus' warning to the lawyers that it is justice and the love of God to which the law must pay attention applies to this generation as it did to his own.

The Problem of the Vacuum

The larger problem is that for years we have been operating in a justice vacuum where not only lawyers but also judges and legislatures have been wary of dealing too forthrightly with questions of justice and ethics that go below the safer level of tactics into those of strategy and ideology. The exaggerated separation of Church and State has contributed to this, as has a host of other attitudes that have made the subject of ethics forbidden in schools and suspect in business, law, medicine and even in the pulpits. The number of courses in ethics being taught in the graduate schools of law and business for example, although improving, is woefully inadequate. We have been going through a period of great ethical silence and it is catching up with us and threatening to destroy us. So it is that now, after the horse has escaped from the barn, educators, jurists and legislators, business people and sociologists, news commentators and national magazines are beginning to recognize the desperate need, as *Time* Magazine put it, "to find our ethical roots." (May 25, 1987)

The fact is that nature and ethics abhor a vacuum. Without a clearly defined and articulated ethic, inevitably attitudes of greed and self-interest move into the vacuum and create an ethic to their own liking. This is what has been happening to us in the last two generations in America. Again, Jesus told a parable that was to the point, for they had the same difficulty in his day. (Luke 11:24-26) He had been healing people, and he compared what was happening within those individuals to a house that had been swept and put in order. In first century terms, the demon had been driven out. But he was determined to return to that house, so he found seven other demons more evil than himself and they entered it and the last state was worse than the first. The problem of the house was its emptiness. There was a desperate need for someone to occupy the house and keep out the demons.

The terrible problem of Jesus' age was its religious and ethical vacuum. He was pointing to the need within men and women for the presence of the sovereign God and a commitment to his justice. Without that, the house, the person, the society would inevitably be filled with the demons of self-interest and greed that always crowd into the vacuum of widespread atheism. Today a similar emptiness has invited the greed merchants to move in and take advantage of this problem-ridden tort law situation. It has enabled clever plaintiffs and trial lawyers who know a lot about the loopholes and bizarre opportunities to exploit the system with what one might call "creative greed litigation."

The antidote seems plain. George Will said it well in a recent *Washington Post* column: "The central question of American life concerns the moral limits on...the pursuit of happiness." It is an ethical crisis, and we are ill-prepared for it. As one who has taught ethics at the college level for 35 years, it is my observation that the level of ethical education is the lowest of all subjects upon which one might test students upon entrance into college. Nowhere is this more plain than in a study of the legal profession, despite the significant efforts of many dedicated jurists. The entire legal community, including the legislatures, needs to be brought out of the box of the law, out of its ethical vacuum into a new confrontation with the ethics of justice, if the law is to be totally adequate in its application.

Distorted Justice: A Legislative Problem

But now let's be more specific. What do we mean by justice when applied within the legal process? One answer is to see what it is not. A recent bulletin of the Ohio Association of Civil Trial Attorneys observed that "recent trends show that the system is out of balance and that litigation leads to manifestly unfair results." The evidence presented in this book would seem to confirm this judgment. The problem is not only one of achievement, but of direction. Our concepts of justice at certain points have become ethically skewed by the prevailing mentality of individualism, hedonism and atheism, providing another particularly fertile ground for the operation of the Greed Syndrome. There are several current attitudes becoming either legislative fiat or legal precedent which illustrate and contribute to this situation. It is with these that we come to the details of this deeper philosophical problem.

From Each According to His Ability:
Responsibility and Fault

In an article in *Forbes* Magazine (Aug. 11, '86, 79) entitled "The Tort Reform Quagmire," Richard Greene makes a telling point: "For generations, liability in America was indeed keyed to fault, with the idea being that individuals had to assume some of the responsibility for the risks of simply being alive. But in the last decade or so, a weird sort of socialism has crept into tort law, as judges have begun to hold that anyone who suffers harm ought to be entitled to damages from someone, no matter whether the person paying the money is truly at fault. The crux of the legal issue is whether we want a pure compensatory liability system or one based on true fault."

There is ample evidence to support this observation. What is happening at an ethical level is that the social climate of recent years has distorted our concept of justice. In its laudable concern to make people responsible for the victim, the courts have ignored other aspects of the justice of God. Not only does the bias toward the victim violate the universal love of God, but the whole adversary system destroys human relationships and tends to reject any concern for forgiveness and reconciliation.

Perhaps the most significant principle involved in this debate is that which makes the ability to pay rather than fault the basic criterion for deciding who foots the bill in a product liability suit. It is technically called the "principle of strict liability"; more popularly dubbed "the deep pocket principle." The one who has the deepest pocket must pay. This is what Harry Featherstone and the Will Burt Company got caught in. His concern was survival. Ours has to do more with the ethical viability of this principle. It is a very complex philosophical question and in its larger context involves the ethical meaning of responsibility itself and how the Hebrew-Christian ethic deals with the problem of fault or blame.

From a Biblical standpoint, responsibility for others is an extension of the concept of the love of God as it is strengthened by the imperative of God's law which commands us to love one another. When applied to public policy this has demanded that responsibility be placed where it will effectively reduce hazards to society. The purpose of this concept of strict liability is to protect the consumer by removing defective products from the market place. From an ethical standpoint, it is saying that we all must be as responsible as we are able to be for the welfare of our brother and sister. This is ostensibly a Christian statement and one can find support for it in the Bible. Jesus told a parable about a "faithful and wise steward," concluding with the statement, "To whom much is given, of him will much be required." (Luke 12:42-48) In The Acts of the Apostles (2:45) we find the disciples selling their possessions and distributing them to all, "as any had need." From each according to his ability, to each according to his need. This is the Christian principle which was exploited by Karl Marx and which seems to lie behind the concept of strict liability.

The problem here is that these passages are being lifted out of context and made to stand alone as a basic social policy. Put into the total context of the sovereignty and justice of God, where Jesus, Paul and Luke would have intended it, the love of God is never out of touch with the wrath of God. Responsibility and fault are the two sides of this ethical coin. Fault is the necessity for punishment which is an expression of the wrath of God. It is intensely personal. For Jesus, as for the prophets before him, God's wrath was always, at its center, a description of a broken relationship, the divine reaction to the personal rejection of his grace. And this demands punishment for individuals who reject his will. Wrath is the highly selective punishment of individual fault. God's punishment comes to those individuals who deserve his reproof for they are at fault. The principle of strict liability, or "deep pocket," violates the concept of justice being developed here for it deprives fault of its personal, selective, situational character. Those who are not at fault, or only minimally so, are forced to bear the blame. This is unjust.

Responsibility and fault, to be just, must also be part of law and freedom which round out the Biblical concept of justice. Here is another crucial problem. When love and wrath and the concepts of responsibility and fault which stem from them are made into law, there is a built-in danger of theological and ethical distortion. The great danger with this particular deep pocket principle is that law has eclipsed the preservation of our freedom. To say that we must be willing to pay for damage to others irrespective of the extent of our fault denies us the individuality and freedom which is our birthright within the Biblical concept of justice. This is responsibility without fault, which is love without wrath, and law without freedom. From this standpoint, it is clearly an unjust principle. The many efforts to legislate it out of existence are a widespread recognition of this ethical fact.

"To Each According to His or Her Need"

This is also an important Christian strategy that has been skewed in its recent application. Greed is not need. Vengeance is not need. Exploitation of the system for personal advantage is not need. This principle is only valid when under the total discipline of God's justice: his love, his wrath, his command, his insistence on our freedom. When this or any other Biblical principle is lifted out of the total context of God's sovereignty and justice, then it turns to injustice and produces a rash of bizarre and pathological symptoms such as we have been seeing in the explosion of the Greed Syndrome within the courts.

The Defendant Will Always Lose to the Victim

This bit of legal hyperbole coming out of Harry Featherstone's interview with one of the judges in the Will Burt case, whether literally or even partially true, violates the universality of this ethic where justice must be equally for all. Law has an important place in the protection of the weak, the poor and the innocent; but it must also apply to the strong, the rich, and the guilty. The scales of justice would seem to be sorely tilted today in favor of the plaintiff and the poor. If this is true, it is unjust.

The ethic of the Bible demands our concern for the underdog; but this must not be as a product of injustice to others. The judge's response to Featherstone's question would seem to be a reflection within some courts of the current debate over affirmative action with its acceptance of temporary injustice in favor of an eventual righting of the scales. It is the old problem of ends and means. The ethical danger here is that the ends usually take on and suffer from the quality of the means. If the means are unjust, the ends will also be unjust. In this case, the bias toward the victim would seem to have encouraged the escalation of the Greed Syndrome.

Somebody Else Must Pay For My Trouble

This current attitude has surfaced regularly in this study and is one of the major assumptions fueling the Greed Syndrome. It is an application of the same idea of unconditional love which we have been discussing, which is love without fault. And it is directly contrary to the Hebrew-Christian revelation. God's love is a just love, demanding obedience and chastening disobedience, demanding integrity and condemning greed. God's love places a great burden of responsibility upon us, not only for others, but for ourselves.

God's love makes us responsible for our own actions and will not release us from their consequences. Unconditional love is unjust love and eventually destroys those subject to it. Like an over-indulgent parent, our courts and legislatures have turned away from assigning fault, and so removed this essential condition of individual responsibility. This is eroding the justice of the litigation process.

Such an attitude would also seem to represent a misunderstanding of the wrath of God. Punishment for sin is an essential ingredient in the justice of God. Litigation can and does defend the rights of the defenseless, and those who abuse them must be punished. But wrath must be just and loving, and law must permit human freedom. Our application of wrath has become skewed just like the application of love. Punishment for the sins of the defendant must be matched by a similar concern for the plaintiff and for those who abuse the system. Wrath must be redemptive, rather than an exercise in vengeance. The recent escalation of large awards for punitive damages would seem in many cases to violate this aspect of justice and also give a large opportunity for the Greed Syndrome. Freedom to sue is a fundamental expression of Hebrew-Christian justice; but this must also involve the freedom from suit, which has been radically curtailed in recent years.

What we seem to be experiencing in our courts is a laudable attempt to implement certain Hebrew-Christian principles of concern for the under-privileged, a desire to punish offenders and to right the social imbalances of our time in favor of minorities and the oppressed. The problem is that these efforts have not gone far enough with the ethical tradition which demands justice for all, love balanced with wrath, law in proper relation to freedom. Without this total balance, we have, by default, though perhaps with the highest intentions, produced a lopsided kind of justice which is really injustice. This has provided a ready climate for the aggressive intrusion of special interest groups and for greedy individuals skillful at exploiting the justice box, the justice vacuum, the justice imbalance we have been examining.

Tort Reform Ferment

The greatest remedial activity comes at the tactical, short term level as many groups attempt to apply first aid to this situation. The American Bar Association has formed a 14 member action commission to improve the tort liability system. Over 300 trade associations in the nation have banded together to form the National Product Liability Alliance to fight for economic justice. Trial lawyers, now on the defensive, have formed an Alliance for Consumer Rights to resist groups like HALT (Help Abolish Legal Tyranny), a Washington-based organization claiming 100,000 members and dedicated to reforming the civil justice system. Every state in the union has legislation pending on one or another aspect of the problem. Ohio, for example, has recently redefined "intentional" tort in workers' compensation. At the federal level, Congress has considered more than 50 bills addressing these issues, like that of Senator Bob Kasten (R-Wis) to replace conflicting state laws with a national product liability code.

The most basic and far-ranging legislation is that which challenges the principle of no-fault, like that of Dan Glickman (D-Kans) which would limit general aviation liability by allocating damages according to fault alone without regard to ability to pay. This is akin to the move to replace the rule of joint and several liability which is behind the deep pocket principle. Legislatures in Kansas, New Mexico, New Hampshire, Vermont and Ohio have already eliminated or modified that principle. Some, like Ohio, have substituted absolute liability with "proportionate liability," where no litigant "is compelled to make contributions beyond his or her own proportionate share of the entire liability."

Many other suggestions are emerging, such as fining plaintiffs and lawyers for introducing frivolous suits, or, like the English Rule, where the loser pays the winner's costs. Others are working at the elimination of the contingency fee system of payment for lawyers which can amount to 40 percent or more of the money awarded to the plaintiff. It is often pointed out that America is the only nation on earth permitting this kind of fee system. Putting a cap on awards, or on lawyers' fees, punishing lawyers who use various legal techniques to pad their bills, or making punitive damage awards go to the state instead of the plaintiff, are some of the many legislative efforts being made to bring this epidemic of greed under control.

"Settle With Your Adversary on the Way" (Luke 12:58; Matt. 5:25)

Roger Fisher, who is an expert in negotiation and the non-litigious settlement of disputes, insists that in his long experience, "from the point of view of the parties to a lawsuit, the costs are in vain; almost every litigated case is a mistake...We could settle the case together, even before it is filed, for roughly the same amount as the final judgment...If we had worked side by side with the other party, we could have agreed on a creative solution that served our interests far better than any judgment a court might order." He points out that we are suffering from a lawyer's perception of what constitutes the normal way to deal with disputes. Instead, he and many others are proposing creative alternatives to litigation, like mediation, or minitrials. In 16 states, cases in which damages are under $15,000-$25,000 go to an arbitration proceeding with the right to trial if one doesn't accept the award. The American Arbitration Association promotes mediation of auto-injury disputes and reports settlements in 90 per cent of such cases. Private firms also offer help. EnDispute of Washington D.C., for a small fee, helps arrange a private, voluntary settlement conference before a neutral adjudicator, usually a retired judge.

As reported in *U.S. News and World Report*, (Jan. 27. '86, 35f.) Judge Thomas Lambros, of Cleveland, has designed the "short jury trial," featuring a half day trial before six jurors who hear arguments from both sides with no live testimony from witnesses. Most parties settle on the basis of the jury's advice. All of this is very hopeful; but it is just beginning and is very controversial. It also tends to deal with tactics instead of strategies, with details instead of ethics, with short term emergency symptoms instead of the deeper strategic and ideological causes of the litigation crisis. To make these hopeful new tactics work in ways that go below symptoms to causes will take a radical change in attitude at the deepest level.

Jesus proposed a more profound, sweeping and permanent antidote to the litigious rancor that is poisoning our nation. When he commanded his followers to "make friends quickly with your accuser, while you are going with him to court," (Matt. 5:25) he was not only giving the kind of good advice proposed by Roger Fisher and others, he was proposing a radical reorientation of their lives. His command to avoid litigation by settling out of court was part of the Sermon on the Mount, a summary of his entire ethical teaching. It comes to focus with the command to "seek first the kingdom of God and his righteousness," and is crystallized elsewhere in his summary of the law and the prophets: "Love the lord your God with all your heart and soul and mind and strength, and your neighbor as yourself." (Mark 12:28-34) This was Jesus' basic approach to handling disputes, to dealing with enemies and being angry with your brother or sister. What he was doing was offering a new way, beyond the legalism of his day, to a redis-

covery of the old prophetic call for justice, along with a new
and exciting revelation of God's love in himself: "You have
heard it said of old, 'You shall not kill'; but I say unto you,
everyone who is angry with his brother shall be liable to judgment...love your enemies...make friends with your accuser."
Here is the tactical expression of the loving justice of God.

The current rash of litigation, the legalistic attitudes within
the law, the motivations within plaintiffs who immediately leap
to litigation to solve disputes and promote their own interests,
are profoundly at variance with the ethic of love and justice
proposed by Jesus and the Old Testament prophets. We stand
under judgment, not only before the law of the land, but before
the justice of God. The rash of litigation, with all that accompanies it, is clear evidence of that judgment already in
progress.

Chapter 8

I Must Not Suffer

"Angry Baby Doctors Threaten Revolt" was the headline in a recent UPI article from Boston. Obstetricians threatened to stop accepting new patients despite pleas from the governor. In Dillon, Montana, it is reported that 80 per cent of the obstetricians are leaving obstetrics. (Charles Kuralt, NBC, 12/27/87) This phenomenon is being repeated in Florida and Nevada and in many other parts of the country. (CBS News, 6/30/87) In the small Ohio college town of Wooster, there used to be 17 OBs listed in the phone book. Now there are five. It is almost impossible in some parts of the country to find a nurse-midwife. Physicians in many high risk specialties have ceased to practice. More and more doctors are refusing to treat certain types of patients, especially those who are transients and in a high risk category. Doctors are angry at lawyers; patients are angry at doctors. Once some of the most highly respected professionals, doctors, along with lawyers, are the target of widespread antagonism and resentment. Again, one wonders what is happening in this nation with one of the most highly developed medical professions on earth.

The most obvious thing is that the cost of medical care has taken off into the blue. In 1925, America's total health care bill was $4 billion. In recent years it has increased 12 per cent per year. By 1988, it had risen to approximately $500 billion, over

10 percent of the GNP. Everyone is angry about it, especially the 37 million who have no medical insurance. Not only are doctors some of the highest paid professionals, but many, like the obstetricians in Boston, are complaining that even their inflated incomes (average $121,410 after expenses) are not enough to make it possible or worthwhile for them to practice.

In fairness to the doctors, one must recognize that it is much more costly to practice medicine than it used to be. For example, first year tuition for in-state students at public medical schools is up 108 per cent on average since 1980. It is common today for medical students to emerge from graduate school $30,000 to $60,000 in debt, with an additional cost of $50,000 to $150,000 to begin a practice. Average annual professional expenses increased from $38,500 in 1975 to $92,600 in 1984, and they continue to rise. (*U.S. News & World Report*, Jan. 26, '87, 44f.)

The largest single cost for doctors is that of malpractice insurance. The number of medical malpractice cases rose 362 per cent from 1978 to 1985. (*Forbes*, Aug. 11, '86, 79) The average total insurance premium for all doctors listed in the most recent census abstract grew from $5800 in 1982 to $8400 in 1984. The highest are obstetricians who paid an average of $10,000 in 1982 and $18,000 in 1984. On Long Island, in 1984, it was $68,000. In 1985 the rate rose to over $100,000 in New York, and since then has continued to escalate. In Miami, it has rocketed to a reported $167,000. Not untypical of the hospital situation is that of one Cleveland hospital. For years, its malpractice premium stayed around $100,000. In the last three years, it has risen to $750,000 per year for the same coverage. The average salary of a midwife is $25,000; but the cost of insurance is often more than the annual salary. It is estimated that the average cost to the patient to insure the doctor or the hospital is about 15 per cent of the total bill. At times it is much higher. A classic illustration is the DTP serum which has largely eradicated diphtheria, whooping cough and tetanus in America. In a recent invoice supplied by a local physician, the charge per dose was $3.40 for the vaccine and $8.00 for "liability surcharge." This is another of those strange anomalies that seem to characterize our economy at this particular time.

The Malpractice Epidemic

Behind these surface phenomena lie a welter of causes that not only represent a special case of hyperlexia, but also the activity of the Greed Syndrome within the practice of medicine. Both a symptom and a cause is the epidemic of malpractice litigation that has hit the nation. According to a *Forbes* magazine study, between 1978 and 1985, the number of medical malpractice cases increased 362 per cent, from 385 to 1779. Dr. Donovan Baumgartner, president of the Ohio Medical Association, reported that in this state nearly 50 per cent of all doctors have been sued. The way it works is that doctors themselves fix the standard for care, and if that is not met one is liable for malpractice. But, according to Baumgartner, in practice "anything short of perfection makes you liable." Awards, too, are exploding with about 21 per cent of the cases recovering over $50,000, and some in the millions. As Charles Kuralt put it in reporting on the case of the Dillon, Montana, obstetricians, "We have become a sue-happy society."

One of the characteristic features of this new situation is the unusual and even peculiar nature of some of the suits. In New Hampshire, for example, a doctor was sued for failing to inform the parents about the potential damage of rubella to their unborn child, and the advisability of an abortion. The child should not have been born, and they contended the fault was the doctor's. This was allowed to go to the jury, and it resulted in a new tort, that of "wrongful life."

An Ohio judge reports the case of a 33 year old woman who was brain damaged as a result of an error in anesthesia. The case was settled with the doctor for $5 million, but the parents also sued, claiming damages for loss of their daughter's love and affection. *U.S. News and World Report* finds in its research that emotional distress is becoming an increasingly valid tort. The fear of becoming ill is itself considered an acceptable cause for suit. The Rock Hudson AIDS case is one of the most recent high-profile illustrations. The plaintiff, Hudson's lover, received a reported $22 million judgment, most of which was for the pain and suffering of not knowing if he would sometime in the future contract AIDS, even though he tested negative at the time of the trial.

Charles Landefeld, Cleveland defense lawyer specializing in hospital litigation, sees evidence of this epidemic of litigation in the scarcity of the vaccine DTP. Heretofore, three companies have produced this serum. Because of the rash of litigation, however, two have discontinued distribution. The result has been a shortage of the basic serum. The problem is dramatized by the statistics which Landefeld has amassed. In 1978, there were close to 18 million doses of this vaccine distributed, and one lawsuit was filed with a claim for $10 million. In 1984, there were 16 million doses given, 73 lawsuits were filed, and 28 asked for damages totalling 1.3 billion. In 1985, 19.7 million doses were dispensed. There were 219 lawsuits filed, and the damages sought in only 120 of these were over $3 billion, more than 30 times the value of all the DTP vaccines sold that year. To continue selling the product exposed the company to liability 30 times the market value of the vaccine, so they ceased distributing the product. The shortage of vaccine, and the increased risk of the resurgence of diphtheria, whooping cough and tetanus, would seem to be traceable directly to the rash of malpractice litigation we are describing.

The ripple effect of this malpractice fever has spread throughout the medical profession. The increase of defensive medicine is an inevitable result. More aggressive patient management, more caesarean sections in place of natural births, more expensive testing and consultation are all widespread and, according to The Ohio State Medical Association, add from $15 to $40 billion to our annual cost of health care.

Equally distressing is the warfare that has developed between doctors and lawyers. It was reported over *20/20* (Dec. 30, '87) that some California doctors had declared war on malpractice lawyers by subscribing to a service called "Medical Alert." Through this, computers keep track of every patient who sues a doctor, and these are subsequently refused treatment. Lawyers retaliated by setting up a similar service, with the name of every doctor who is sued. These are made available to potential patients. Perhaps most distressing is the deterioration of relations between patients and doctors, traditionally one of trust, respect and often affection. The statistics don't reveal the destructive anguish which is present when a patient sues a doctor who has been working, whether skillfully or not, for the patient's welfare to the best of his or her ability.

Diagnosing the Malpractice Fever

It would seem that the American medical profession itself is sick, and there is an urgent need to go below surface symptoms to the causes of this malady. In analyzing the situation, one must begin by recognizing that America is on a health kick of major proportions. Health is "in," and we have been convinced that we not only can, but must live a comfortable, beautiful, pain-free life. The number of doctors and the superabundance of hospitals, clinics, health spas, health literature, TV programs and health research give dramatic testimony to our worship of the healthy, comfortable body. Between 1950 and 1985, the number of doctors increased from 219,997, to 552,716 and the medical schools continue to be overcrowded. *Dun's Business Month* reports that the nation's hospitals are woefully overbedded. (Feb. '87, Vol. 129, 32f) In my own small town classified telephone directory, there are two pages of attorneys, three pages of clergy and churches, six pages of insurance companies, six pages of doctors, and a total of seventeen pages for all medical services, including doctors, hospitals and other specialized concerns.

Doctors Must Be Perfect

Along with this, which some are calling a "glut of doctors," has gone a marvelous explosion in science and technology that has put America in the forefront of many aspects of medicine. There is good reason for the king of Saudi Arabia to come to the Cleveland Clinic for treatment. But along with these advances have come a host of problems. With new possibilities for life extension, the complete eradication of certain diseases, and a spate of breakthroughs in medicine, have come new ethical dilemmas, and new possibilities for suits. And what is perhaps most to the point, new expectations from the medical profession.

If medical science is so clever, why must I be allowed to suffer? Charles Landefeld points to a sense of scientific perfectionism that plagues the medical community. We have oversold our scientific progress to the point that patients demand infallibility from science. The very success of medical science has led to the assumption that even when doctors warn patients of the risks of a procedure, if something goes wrong, the doctor is to be held accountable because doctors must be perfect.

Professor Laurence VandeCreek counsels with students on ethics at the Ohio State School of Medicine. He reports that, with many patients who have sued their doctors, there is a deep-seated anger that is a product of this excessive expectation. Doctors are supposed to have the answers. When they don't, litigation is a common way to express that anger and frustration. There is an absence of forgiveness as well as common sense in much of our monumental expectation from a science which despite its brilliant successes is still fumbling in the dark.

An Identity Crisis

Another cause of so much malpractice litigation involves the changing image of the profession itself. Is it still an idealistic calling dedicated to healing and service and the welfare of the patient, or is it a business run by professionals whose chief concern is to make a lot of money? The high salaries of doctors contribute inevitably to this latter perception as do the many hospitals run for profit, with their emphasis on the bottom line. Charles Landefeld points to an identity crisis within the medical community, between Norman Rockwell's picture of the old family doctor examining a doll held up by a little girl, and the physician as a technician, a business man or woman, impersonal, efficient, more concerned for you to pay your bill than to be healed. He or she is not a friend, but a potential adversary, especially if things go wrong, or if you don't pay your bill. Landefeld attributes the escalation of the malpractice crisis to this radical change in the traditional image of the doctor, along with a severe deterioration of doctor-patient relationships.

Beyond this, one can point to the changes in the justice system and the practice of law detailed in the last chapter, especially the shared risk concept, with the erosion of the necessity to prove fault. The bias of the courts toward the plaintiff has opened the door to a firestorm of litigation where these biases and loopholes are exploited without mercy. One of the chief targets is the nation's physicians. Ohio Appeals Judge J.R. Milligan points especially to the landmark case of *Avellone vs. St. John's Hospital* as the beginning salvo in opening up medical litigation. Historically, it had been held in common that charitable hospitals were not liable for their negligence. This case abolished that immunity because "the social consciousness of our society is different than when the immunity law was first drafted." Hospitals, doctors and the entire medical profession are now seen by more and more people as no longer engaging in a charitable enterprise but in a business, and so they should be treated as such.

The major fuel behind this litigation holocaust is the high availability of insurance. There is a very deep pocket out there. It belongs to a host of impersonal companies whose rates are said to be too high, and who are suspected by some of possessing collectively the largest accumulation of wealth on earth. So let's make the insurance companies pay.

The Greed Syndrome: Who's to Blame?

Health mania, over-expectations from medical science, anger at imperfect doctors, suspicion of the new business images of doctors and hospitals, encouragement from the many alterations in the justice system, the temptation to exploit huge insurance pockets: these are some of the ingredients in the malpractice fever. But the virus which sets them all aflame is the same Greed Syndrome we have been observing in other segments of our society.

First, there are greedy plaintiffs, lots of them. In a New York court, a woman sued her obstetrician for "wrongful birth." (*CMS Journal*, Winter, '86, 19) It seems she had tubal ligation surgery because she had three children and didn't want any more. A year later, she became pregnant again, so she sued the doctor for malpractice. What she was saying was, "If you had done your job right, we wouldn't have had this little girl. So you must pay the cost of raising her until the age of 18." By not choosing an abortion, the doctor had violated her right to privacy. Two lower courts refused to award the couple child support, but their lawyers vowed to take it to the Supreme Court.

One case reports a 34 year old man who sued his doctor because of failure to diagnose and prevent a heart attack. Though he recovered and was able to jog, swim, ski and ride a bicycle, he estimated his life was shortened by 10 years. He won damages of $1.3 million, which consisted of $800,000 actual damages, and $500,000 for pain and suffering. The latter was reduced by the trial court to $250,000. The man appealed this reduction as far as the Supreme Court, which refused to hear the case.

There are, of course, many legitimate malpractice claims, and patients need this protection. But my research reveals that, given the present situation, the factor of greed is operating vigorously.

Insurance companies tend to point to greedy lawyers, and there is some evidence for this. A responsible source reports that in one large hospital lawyers have been seen going from bed to bed asking patients, in effect, if there is not something for which they wish to sue their doctors. It is clear that in medical cases for every $1.00 of insurance recovered, 30 cents goes to the injured patient, and 70 cents for legal and administrative costs. The ABA deplores these abusive practices, and is concerned to reduce the cost of legal services, and so the incentive behind them. They do exist frequently enough to warn us of the aggressive determination of some lawyers to misuse the malpractice system.

The other side of the coin is that there are also greedy doctors and hospitals who take advantage of patients. One unusual case involves a surgeon whose colleague called him a "medical buccaneer." He is under investigation in a private hospital for performing unnecessary operations. By practicing his specialty of spinal surgery, he made $750,000 in one year, and the hospital over $2 million, performing a record 340 such operations. It is reported that clever salesmen and greedy doctors can make over a million a year on pacemakers installed unnecessarily.

Blue Cross and Blue Shield of Ohio has, on at least two occasions, launched an attack against soaring hospital costs in Greater Cleveland, charging that hospitals have reaped huge profits from Medicare. A study by an accountant firm showed 33 regional hospitals receiving a $96 million profit in Medicare payments in 1985, and 13 city hospitals had $64 million in surplus. These cases are certainly not typical, but they are part of this upsurge of greed we are describing. And the problem seems to be escalating. A special report by ABC News (2/13/89) reveals that heart by-pass surgery increased from 170,000 in 1982 to 332,000 in 1987, and that questions are now being raised within the medical community as to the possibility that more and more of this is unnecessary. This documentary details that some hospitals are offering incentives to doctors to send them candidates for heart surgery in order to fight for their share of the lucrative by-pass market.

Some Attempts at Therapy

To help meet these problems, many doctors are turning to what is sometimes called "sheltered medicine": health maintenance organizations, and walk-in clinics like Health Stop which has 35 clinics in the Boston area. Blue Cross, Blue Shield are setting up health care plans. Doctors are joining group clinics to cut costs, and many other forms of corporate health care are providing a kind of capitalist equivalent to socialized medicine. These plans would all include collective malpractice insurance.

Other legal and legislative remedies are being proposed like that of the California Supreme Court which in 1985 upheld a cap on awards against doctors. The U.S. Supreme Court left standing a California law limiting lawyer's fees in medical malpractice cases. Florida also passed such a law, limiting malpractice awards to $100,000.

To help meet the problem of greedy doctors and hospitals, the president of the American Heart Association is now recommending that patients always seek an independent second opinion when told they need heart by-pass surgery, because of the growing evidence that some hospitals and surgeons are recommending this expensive procedure unnecessarily in order to increase their cash flow. (ABC News, 2/13/89)

The Ethical Dimension

So far, the symptoms, causes and remedies we have discussed have been fairly superficial. There is a lot of defensive posturing and blaming of plaintiffs, lawyers, insurance companies, hospitals and doctors that goes on in this discussion. There is also a rash of Band-Aid legislation without really coming to grips with the deeper causes of the illness. I am not concerned to single out any one group for blame because that would be unfair and also fruitless. Greed is everywhere and the climate for its operation consists of widespread social attitudes in which we are all involved. The usual symptoms of the Greed Syndrome are here, but there is something else that makes this a special case.

There is a new element to American hedonism that comes to a head in the medical area. The two points of focus in the ellipse of traditional hedonism are those of seeking pleasure and avoiding pain. Within American hedonism, this translates into two ethical strategies: "I must have it all," and "I must not suffer." It is around these two centers that the malpractice infection festers, and the treatment lies at a deep ethical level.

I Must Have It All

The first generation of affluence in any society takes affluence with gratitude and humility as it remembers the bad old days. The second generation takes their affluence for granted, for they tend to live on the moral capital of their parents. The third generation of affluence takes this as their right, for they have known nothing else and, like the ancient Greek civilization, have abandoned the morals of fathers and mothers in their enjoyment of the fruits of parental dedication. We are living in this third period of post-WorldWar II affluence, and our attitudes clearly reflect it. My research reveals that it is widely believed that we have a right to expect the best. We have a right to use the courts to redistribute the wealth. We have a right to be recompensed for any inconvenience without concern for fault. We have a right to expect doctors to be perfect. And all this gives us a right to seek immediate redress in the courts.

Aside from the arrogance and unreality of this secret and widely held assumption, there is a whole host of ethical problems. One is raised forcefully by Charles Landefeld: "Shall society subjugate the interest of the majority to the interest of the minority of injured patients?" In effect, he is asking whether my demand to have it all, in this case, to be free from all risk, is to be gained at the expense of others? Or does love demand that we apply the principle of the greatest good for the greatest number? He applies this to the case of the polio vaccine. There are some 50 cases of polio annually which result from the administration of the vaccine. There is some risk. But without the use of the serum, it is estimated there would be 50,000 new cases each year. Should the remedy be abolished because of the risk to the few or should it be retained because of the risk to the many?

The same question occurs in the reduction of the availability of the DTP vaccine because the few who have suffered have sued for damages so large that the manufacturers can no longer afford the insurance. Surely there is a middle way here where actual injury can be recompensed without destroying the chances of countless others. There is a need for restraint and a consideration for the rights of the whole of society which some malpractice litigation tends to ignore. Here is another symptom of the injustice characteristic of the Greed Syndrome.

I Must Not Suffer: The Aspirin Generation

We are a nation addicted to pain killers from the more innocuous aspirin and its dozens of substitutes to the more lethal hard drugs. We don't want any pain and suffering. This attitude has become part of the American mystique. It is one of the major ethical strategies that guides this hedonistic culture, and I suspect is one of the deeper causes of the drug explosion. We have become a soft culture, lulled by our affluence into an addiction to comfort. The quality of our education testifies to our aversion to demanding hard work from ourselves and others in the schools. Our low level of physical fitness testifies to our love for indulgence and hatred of the kind of physical pain and self-discipline that any athlete knows is required to excel in sports. The immorality of both old and young testifies to the lack of discipline and punishment in the home. We are fat and soft and morally out of condition and have become a target for all those who are dedicated to exploiting the weakness and moral immaturity of a culture that has become addicted to a love of luxury and a hatred of pain and suffering.

And now we are in the third generation after the Great War. Our love of the good life has become hardened into a right where, instead of wanting and pursuing comfort, we are now demanding it in the courts. Suffering is unjust, and violates our civil rights. We have a right to sue in order to compensate for it. The escalation of pain and suffering awards testifies to this modern climate.

The Ethical Problem: A Biblical View

Do we indeed have a right to a life free of suffering, and does this popular strategy strengthen or weaken the moral fibre of our nation? The thesis of these pages is that not only does it weaken us and make us the victim of exploitation and mediocrity, but it is an unjust attitude itself and directly counter to the Hebrew-Christian ethic we have been examining. One of the basic ethical strategies stemming from the sovereignty of God is that putting God first in one's life implies that there are things worse than death and more important than human life. These are the things of the spirit, of justice, of integrity, of honesty and freedom and love. Our priorities, instead, have been an intense fixation upon the supreme importance of physical life. This quickly becomes prostituted into a mania for comfort and the desperate avoidance of pain.

Furthermore, we are a culture which in recent generations has rejected the wrath of God. During and just after World War II, Karl Barth, Reinhold Niebuhr and a number of other theologians were effective in reminding us of this dimension of God's justice. But the years of affluence and the progressive softening of our moral fibre have wiped it out. We have opted instead for a grandfather God who indulges us without condition and who represents more the image of a department store Santa Claus than the awesome deity of the Bible. We have created a lopsided justice where love and permissiveness have overbalanced the wrath and restraint of the Biblical God. We are paying dearly for this unjust situation.

More exactly, ours is a lopsided understanding of God's wrath. We have accepted the need for punishment for sin. Indeed, part of the malpractice problem is the excessive concern for penalty to the endangering of the freedom from suit that is also part of Biblical justice. But then, in this popular theology, we have rejected the other aspect of God's wrath which is his willingness to allow us to suffer, to struggle, to experience pain and calamity and death. The problem of evil is considered by some to be the chief American theological problem. Of course. It is the inevitable product of this inadequate theology. If our only understanding of God is that he is a "good God," then we are led to ask, why all the trouble in the world?

Our God Is Too Small

The Bible gives us a different picture of God's justice. Love and wrath, reward and punishment, blessing and cursing, life and death, success and failure, comfort and pain, prosperity and adversity: these are all elements of God's justice and righteousness. To live as if all of these are not part of life and at times a necessary ingredient in our own spiritual health, is to live in an unreal world. It is to condemn ourselves to the immaturity that comes from rejecting life as it is and living in a fantasy world. Disneyland again.

Elizabeth Kübler-Ross has documented the strange inability of Americans to face up to death in her book, *On Death and Dying*. Her research and willingness to suffer the disapproval of her peers have helped to gain us a breakthrough into a new maturity in facing this crisis. Bregman points to two basic attitudes toward death and dying recognized by Kübler-Ross: that of suffering as injustice, and suffering as loss. In order for the patient or the family to go from an immature, destructive rejection of death to a more mature, productive one of peace and acceptance, they must go beyond the complaints about the injustice of death to an acceptance of the reality of this loss as part of life. I would add that it is an inevitable, natural and beautiful part of a balanced universe created by a just God. One of the chief problems of suffering is not the pain, but the rejection of the pain. The refusal to accept it as part of the natural order of things, and so to make the best and the most of it is the problem. This does not rule out doctors and pain killers and litigation in the search for dignity and justice. But it does caution us against expecting more from life than we have a right to expect.

The God of infinite love has not promised to remove pain and suffering; instead he has promised to give us strength to overcome them, and to put them in perspective. We suffer because we are created with a large and sensitive brain in a universe that operates according to certain physical laws. Suffering is the price of our humanity and of an orderly cosmos. It is only bad if we make it so by refusing to accept it and failing to make the best of it. The attitude that dominates the malpractice courts that somehow suffering, calamity and even inconvenience are unjust, that we have a right to sue somebody else for our trouble, is a reflection of personal immaturity and a lopsided, inadequate view of the nature of reality as created by a just God.

So Let's Sue God

But we don't want to accept this. Note the logic that has emerged in this study: I have a right to a trouble-free, suffering-free, risk-free existence. If I suffer, then someone else must pay. But God has created a world where suffering and trouble are possible and risk is inevitable. This means that either there is no such God and we are all alone in a hostile universe where we must pay primary attention to our own survival, or, if there is a God, then he is unjust, and we have a right to call him to account. All this means that I must take charge of my own justice, and litigation is the most effective route.

The only true evil in this world is men and women rebelling against God. Pain, hardship and suffering are part of a just creation. These only become evil when we refuse the resources which God has offered, enabling us to take the seemingly bad with the good, and emerge victoriously from either as mature sons and daughters of him whose loving justice is beyond anything we are able to comprehend.

Chapter 9

I Must Be Safe

The liability crisis is a two-way battle between defendants and plaintiffs on the one hand, and lawyers and insurance companies on the other. The financial burden falls chiefly on the insurers, for, aside from the government, they have the deepest pockets of all. How deep, it is difficult to tell, for they have carefully avoided divulging their total assets. Ralph Nader and the National Insurance Consumers Organization (NICO) complained recently that the net worth of insurance companies rose more than 300 per cent during the first quarter of 1986, to around $300 billion, with Aetna 348 per cent and Ohio Casualty 317 per cent. It is reported that the property and casualty insurance industry alone made $5.7 billion in profits in the first half of 1986, up from $900 million for the same period in 1985, according to the Insurance Information Institute. Some states, like Ohio, are writing new insurance laws requiring disclosure, so this condition of secrecy may be changing.

The most apparent symptom of hyperlexia and the Greed Syndrome within the insurance industry is the unbelievable escalation of premium costs. A classic case is the aviation industry. In testifying before the House Committee on Transportation, Edward W. Stimpson, president of General Aviation Manufacturers Association, reported that the industry's insurance bill had grown an average of 500 per cent since 1981.

A few companies have had increases of 2,000 and 3,000 per cent in the last four years. In an industry whose 1985 safety record was its best in 20 years, officials are baffled that some senior managing engineers must spend as much as half their time on product liability matters. In the light of the general mood of hyperlexia, perhaps this is not such a mystery.

Piper and Cessna, for example, went out of the small plane business because a plane whose basic cost was $15,000, required an added $80,000 for insurance. Roberta Thompson, president of Aviation Sales Inc., a manufacturer of small corporate and personal aircraft in Miamisburg, Ohio, fears that the entire industry may be fading away. As reported in *The Cleveland Plain Dealer* (Oct. 12, '86), the number of flying schools in the Dayton area has declined in the last five years from eight to two because insurance premiums jumped from $64,500 in 1983 to $143,000 in 1986. What scares Thompson is what this is doing to the development of new technology. "Once they come up with something new, it opens them up to liability on their prior products."

Insurance lawyer Philip Howes reports that tens of thousands of new types of insurance claims are filed each day. This makes insurance companies nervous to the point that some firms can't get coverage at any affordable price. Jim Jubak documents this at length in his article in *Venture*, "Your Premium or Your Company." (Feb. 1986, 40f.) Chuck Slusarcyk is president of CGS Aviation Inc., maker of ultralight aircraft. His insurer cancelled his insurance, and he couldn't find anyone to insure him. As a result, he was unable to get capital to expand, or even a bank loan to finance raw material, and his employees dwindled from 27 to two.

It is reported that no American companies now manufacture protective equipment for hockey because of the high cost of insurance. Eighteen U.S. companies used to make football helmets. Only two are left today. They pay more for liability insurance and legal costs than for material, labor and overhead combined. One could multiply such cases indefinitely. C.W. Bollinger, Montclair, N.J., insurance broker, calls this the worst product liability crisis he has seen in the thirty years he has been in the business. The epidemic of litigation is prompting a radical rise in the cost of insurance, forcing companies out of business, and causing many to "go bare" without insurance, leaving themselves open sometimes to enormous risk. Some communities have either had their insurance cancelled, or can't afford the premiums for what is available, causing them to curtail all kinds of services, such as parks, recreation facilities, and school athletic programs. In Newark, city officials chose to go bare rather than pay $252,000 per year in premiums. Columbus, Dayton and Cleveland have all gone without general liability insurance which protects them against such things as lawsuits over accidents in parks.

Who's to Blame

The insurance crisis is an extension of the same hyperlexia we have been describing, so we could point to the entire range of legal, social, economic, ethical and religious causes already discussed. Certainly there are greedy plaintiffs operating aggressively to exploit the ethically favorable situation and the fact that most persons and organizations have some kind of insurance. Everyone wants to dip into this extremely large pocket. *The Chicago Tribune* dramatically illustrates this point. (*Canton Repository*, Oct. 14, 1985) Tommy was a flunky messenger at a Chicago law firm. A public bus and a truck collided, and although no one was killed, 18 passengers were banged up. Tommy saw the accident, and rushed to the scene. Instead of helping the firemen, Tommy slipped through the back door, flopped on a seat and began groaning as if in excruciating pain. The amused firemen saw him, as one said later, "sneaking in the back door while we were taking people off through the front door. He was a pretty good actor."

On another occasion in Chicago, a car slammed into a bus right in front of a tavern. A transportation worker who was there said, "You never saw a tavern clear out like that. They were coming in droves and trying to get on the bus or lying down in the street, yelling 'Whiplash, I got whiplash.'" On still another occasion, police arrived at an elevated train accident and found people shinnying up the elevated structure to get in the accident, risking breaking their necks to fake a broken neck. As any policeman or fireman will tell you, at a big accident involving public transportation, the injury list just keeps growing.

Certainly there are greedy lawyers who contribute to this syndrome. For example, there is the classic, but hardly typical, case reported in the media (11/17/87) of the man seen wearing a priest's collar, going from victim to victim at a Denver plane crash as if to comfort the victims. He was recognized as the lawyer seen doing the same thing at a previous crash and is now being sought for fraud. There is plenty of incentive as long as the contingency fee remains unregulated and the awards unrestrained. The Insurance Services Office of New York stated in its 1976-77 survey of over 23,000 closed claims, "For every dollar paid to a product liability victim, 42 cents was expended in defense by lawyers or related expenses." The U.S. Chamber of Commerce statistics give an updated report that the average product liability award increased from $345,000 to more than $1 million in the last ten years. Lawyers last year received 60 per cent of all awards for asbestos litigation. It has become a cliche that "nobody wins but the lawyers," who are fast becoming public enemy number one in America.

This unfortunate caricature of a noble profession has, whether rightly or wrongly, been enhanced by the aggressive activity of the Plaintiffs Bar Association, an organization dedicated to protecting the injured plaintiff. Through its president, it has insisted there is no product liability crisis in Ohio. Its vigorous opposition to tort and insurance law reform, however, and especially to putting a cap on awards and restraining the practice of contingency fees, tend to give the impression that it is primarily interested in preserving its own exorbitant fee structure. The Ohio Underwriter, for example, an insurance magazine, complained that trial lawyers in New York had begun a campaign to raise $5 million "to blunt the efforts of the insurance business to reform the civil justice system." (Jan, '86)

The Great Insurance Debate

The crux of this debate is the battle between the trial lawyers and the insurance companies. And certainly the Greed Syndrome has been operating within the insurance field, as within all the others. After two years of intensive investigation, on the morning in which these words were written, it was publicly announced that the attorneys general of eight states were filing suit against a handful of insurance companies, including The Hartford, Aetna, Allstate and Lloyds of London. One attorney general called it the most insidious fraud undertaken in recent insurance history.

Charles Brown, Attorney General of California, charged that "profits went up to the level of greed," and this was having "a catastrophic impact on the nation." The charges were that liability insurance was being dangerously restricted by refusing to insure companies and communities and by raising rates to a disastrous level, sometimes representing thousands of percent increase. This was on the basis of what was considered a crisis which the insurance companies had manufactured themselves while loudly proclaiming they were going bankrupt. This small group of companies was also charged with "collusive conduct," so dominating the industry that only a handful of companies could play the game. Since insurance companies have been exempt from anti-trust laws, and not subject to federal regulations on rate increases, this charge of restraining trade would constitute an extension of the anti-trust laws to include insurance. If sustained, it would represent a major change in thinking.

The history of this problem has been monitored for many years. It is often pointed out that the present situation is a product of insurance greed in the past. From 1979 to 1982, high

interest rates transformed the insurance business into what
Mike Mahoney and Thomas Suddes in *The Cleveland Plain
Dealer* called "a go-go industry, richly profitable and steered
toward growth." (Oct 12, '86) There was a lot of money around,
and money market rates had gone beyond 15 per cent, so, like
the large stock brokers, the insurance companies wanted to get
into investment. This came to be known as "cash-flow under-
writing." Insurance carriers wanted all the cash they could get
for high yield investments.

What began was a war among the insurers for premiums,
cutting rates in order to write as much insurance as they could,
often accepting bad risks in order to increase cash flow. Mahoney and Suddes point out that this often meant that premiums
yielded less than the companies had to pay in claims; but for
several years the net investment gain more than made up for
the losses from insurance policies. In 1984, this cash-invest-
ment joy ride caught up with the industry. According to A.M.
Best Co., which rates the financial health of insurance companies, property and casualty insurers were shocked to discover an operating loss of $3.8 billion.

At that point, they began to escalate insurance premiums
and to cut large numbers of insured from their rolls in what
some have called a massive over-reaction to a crisis of their
own creation. Along with this, Lloyds of London decided to get
out of the U.S. market, due to the excess of litigation in this
country. They controlled 30 per cent of the umbrella insurance
which pays for the astronomical awards beyond what the first
layer of normal insurance policies will pay. This further con-
founded an already losing situation. It would seem that, historically, the appearance of greed today in excessive rate
increases is a product of the well-documented greed of yester-
day. They were indeed going bankrupt, but it would appear it
was their own fault, which they are now passing on to their
customers. Along with the whole litigation mania we have
been describing, this has acted to create a crisis within the
insurance industry which is producing some very bizarre
results.

Whose fault is it? As Thomas O'Day of the Alliance of American Insurers is recently reported saying, "There is no point in pinning the blame on any group. We can all share the blame for the mess we're in." And there is truth in this rather defensive statement. The evidence presented in this book shows that the Greed Syndrome is operating vigorously throughout all segments of our society.

Emergency Therapy

Beyond the suggestions for legal reform made in the last chapter, there are many other efforts which apply specifically to the insurance crisis. Perhaps the least helpful is the latest wrinkle coming out of a recent New York air disaster. The insurance companies were reported hiring detectives to frighten claimants by digging up dirt against them to get them to settle out of court. More positive have been efforts like The Insurance Information Institute which sponsored a national symposium on civil justice reform in April, 1986. More partisan would be the efforts of the Ohio Insurance Institute in putting together an advertising campaign, aimed at opinion leaders and the public, deploring the sad condition of the civil justice system. (*Ohio Underwriter*, Jan. '86) More political would be the efforts of "Access to Justice," a California rate-cutting campaign, in putting an initiative on the ballot requiring a 20 per cent lowering of rates for auto and other types of insurance. This materialized in proposition 103 which won in the 1988 election by a substantial margin.

One of the primary criticisms has been the ability of insurance companies to band together to get claims data and set rates, a luxury not available to small businesses. The recent action of the eight attorneys general should be an aid to restoring competition to the insurance industry by putting it, like all other businesses, under the restraints of the anti-trust laws. Another long-range remedy might be some kind of "Trust Initiative" where individuals would have the ability under law to waive their right to sue any particular party. This would have to be carefully controlled lest unscrupulous persons abuse it; but justice would seem to demand that we have the right to allow those who serve us to be protected from the constant threat of suit. In the meantime, many are taking larger deductibles, going without insurance, starting their own insurance companies, or simply going out of business.

Superficially, the situation is getting a little better. Even as this is being written, some of the most extreme anomalies are being modified if not corrected by legislation, or simply by common sense and Yankee ingenuity. But legislation and clever maneuvering will not cure the problem which lies at a much deeper level and is a matter of attitudes.

The Insurance Dilemma

An ethical analysis of the insurance phenomenon must, I think, recognize at least four things. First of all, the concept is a noble one. It is based on the concern to help people find aid and resources in time of need, and has been a notable success in so doing. Second, the wide prevalence of insurance is a modern phenomenon which has burgeoned even in this generation. Third, it is entirely possible that the insurance industry represents the greatest concentration of wealth in America, and possibly in the world. Fourth, there is increasing evidence that the original goals of this high-minded endeavor have in certain cases been prostituted to those of the Greed Syndrome.

The Safety Fixation

The basic issue has become one of absolute safety and the absence of risk. Lewis Lapham, editor of *Harpers* magazine, complains that "We are obsessed with security. It is harder to get into the offices of *The New York Times* than into the Pentagon." The scrubbing of the Challenger space program because of the demands for safety, beyond what the engineers believe is either possible or necessary, is a symptom of a radical change from the pioneering mentality that has nurtured and sustained our country from its inception through World War II. We have become a security-loving, risk-averse society. This, which is an ethical matter, bids fair to condemn us as a nation to the fear-ridden limbo of mediocrity.

One of the driving agents in this change would seem to be the enormous influence of the insurance industry. We have been led to believe that society owes us a risk-free life. I have a right to be reimbursed for any and all trouble, pain and loss, irrespective of fault, and I must have a lifetime warranty on any thing that might threaten my happiness. This Insurance Mentality has, in one way or another, been legislated into law and so pounded into the popular consciousness that it has become an albatross around our necks. It is filled with problems and has made us especially vulnerable to the activity of the Greed Syndrome.

In general, this safety fixation lacks common sense, creating ridiculous and impossible expectations. As Roger Barnet says of product liability litigation, it is "irrational." To begin with, there is no agreement on what we mean by safety or an acceptable level of risk. The Farm and Industrial Equipment Industry magazine, *Implement and Tractor*, examines this issue in some depth, quoting product liability attorney Harry Philo distinguishing between hazard, risk and danger. Hazard is defined as "a condition or circumstance that presents an injury potential." Risk is "the percentage probability of injury," and danger is "the combination of hazard and risk." (April, '83) By these standards, according to Ralph Barnett of Triodyne, "any risk of serious injury or death is unreasonable or unacceptable if practical accident prevention methods could eliminate it. Conversely, a 100 per cent risk of injury can be reasonable and acceptable if the potential injury is minimal and is recognized by the risk-taker." The trouble is that, as Barnett notes, even the basic term "safety" has no uniform definition. None lies in engineering or technology; socially defined standards can change from state to state, county to county and time to time.

A further problem lies with the means of attaining safety, by whatever definition. The farm industrial equipment industry recommends building safety into the product during manufacture. There is much to be said for prevention in any area. Engineers talk, for instance, of designing products with ZMS (Zero Mechanical State), a concept first adopted by the foundry business and now gaining national prominence. The principle is to see to it that all forms of weight, pressure, electrical power or other energy be reduced to zero, or below an injury-causing level, before a person approaches a machine. The main thrust of ZMS is to make it easy to shut off dangerous energies and then to train people to operate safely the machines that use them. The problem is that product liability is basically irrational. In Barnett's words, we are not smart enough to deal with the misuse of a product. "If engineers succumb to the creation of standards which protect against the extreme misuses of our products . . . we maximize cost to every citizen. . . . No known technique or system can guarantee total protection against losing a liability suit."

The popular approach to safety has been through redress in legislatures and courts. One focus has been on manufacturer's design, with OSHA constantly tightening standards for safety devices. But the litigation experience of Ralph Barnett shows that 85 per cent of accidents are caused by the fault of the operator and only 5 per cent by machine design. More safety guards tend to prompt the hiring of less skilled operators or to encourage skilled operators to do what is not safe. Various courts have ruled that the manufacturers of a product made years ago should be liable for not knowing what has only been recently discovered; it is reported that trial lawyers are now using as evidence old patents not manufactured which, if available, would have prevented an accident. A product today must be safe against "any reasonable foreseeable misuse. The manufacturer can be held liable for random unpredictable events. Courts are reluctant to accept voluntary codes of safety, and acceptable codes are regularly manipulated by knowledgeable lawyers; for example, in deciding how far apart the rungs of a ladder must be in order for it to be safe.

Cornpickers are especially dangerous, and this has led to what the industry calls "the Cornpicker Paradigm." The manufacturer should have done one thing or another to protect against the stupidity or misuse of the operator. With cornpickers, the possibilities are endless. In *Implement and Tractor*, it is regularly complained that there is no way you can make a product comply with all the clever, arbitrary conditions lawyers invent for a particular case. A glance through *Trial* magazine reveals the seed bed for much of this "creative litigation." The impression from this research is that the current safety fixation has provided an open door for product liability litigation that is often confused, arbitrary, subject to emotional bias, and dictated not only by a desire to help the helpless but by self-interest. The Greed Syndrome has been operating through the law in this area of safety.

Perfect safety is a myth. It is no doubt created by many factors, but it seems to be promoted by the insurance industry, and often abused by unscrupulous members of the American bar, a profession that is otherwise more and more determined to slow down the operation of the Greed Syndrome within its ranks. The question all this raises is whether or not insurance as we know it today, in its expanded and all-pervasive form, meets a genuine and legitimate need. Or has it been artificially exaggerated to enhance the profits of the richest industry on the face of the globe? And are we trapped in the insurance net unable to extricate ourselves either from this so-called need or from the problems that attend it?

The Justice of It All

On the surface, the escalation of insurance in recent years would seem to be an enterprise true to the Hebrew-Christian ethic, gaining justice for the poor and restitution for the victimized. In many instances, it has done just that. In more recent years, however, it has become a happy hunting ground for greedy plaintiffs, greedy lawyers and greedy insurance companies. At heart, it is only pseudo-Christian. Certainly, the concern for the poor and the hapless is in line with the loving justice of God with its concern to help people find a good life. Beyond that, it stumbles against the greater adequacy of God's total justice. For love demands help and concern for all, and the insurance crisis clearly demands that we take sides in defending the right of the defendant or the plaintiff to the exclusion of the other and dismisses a concern for what our litigation is doing to the community at large. Love provides appropriate rewards for righteousness conditional upon the worthiness of the individual and the justice of the cause. But the current attitude that we have a right to be reimbursed for any and all trouble, irrespective of fault, shifts the focus away from justice to that of self-interest. The concentration on money as the only way to find redress for a wrong represents the prostitution of this loving concern to the cash-oriented mentality that fuels this example of the Greed Syndrome.

Love demands forgiveness, putting the interest of the other before my own right to redress, but the litigation mentality promoted by this whole system forbids forgiveness to function. Love requires that punishment be not vengeful but redemptive in ways that preserve rather than destroy human relationships. But it is a common observation that in court litigation the legacy is usually one of bitterness and divorce with heavy punitive damages adding fuel to the fire. On all these counts, we are dealing with pseudo-love, restricted and distorted by an avalanche of legalized and commercialized self-interest.

The wrath of God demands punishment for sin, and there is a lot of it to be punished in this mess of litigation. But the wrath of God also reminds us that we do not have a right to a risk-free existence. We live in an orderly creation where "the rain falls on the just and the unjust," where we are punished for our own sins, and where "the sins of the fathers are visited upon the children to the third and fourth generation." It is not possible to have a life-time warranty against anything that might threaten our happiness.

In the light of the Biblical ethic, God has given us the freedom of intelligence which enables us to make essential decisions. This freedom inevitably exposes us to risk, and to responsibility for our own actions. There is no way within his justice that we might have a right to be reimbursed for all our trouble, pain and loss, irrespective of fault.

The command of God requires that we seek first his sovereignty and justice. The fixation on safety and a cash redress of wrongs, irrespective of what it might do to others, is an affirmation of the sovereignty, not of God, but of self. It is the logic of materialism, putting self and material things ahead of God and others.

On the grounds of the Hebrew-Christian ethic, the excesses within this "insurance mentality" stand under judgment as a distortion of the very ethic to which so many in the industry are committed. It is just another tired expression of the Greed Syndrome we are describing.

Do Not Be Anxious

Ultimately, the fixation on safety is a result of fear. And it is here that the insurance companies run the greatest risk of taking advantage of the weakness of others. For with the commendable goal of helping us to combat our fears, they have also enhanced our fears beyond the level of a just self-interest to the enrichment of a multi-billion dollar industry. And now that our anxiety level has been excessively raised, they find they cannot supply us with the insurance that is either within our budget or will make us perfectly safe. The whole concept, begun with such high idealism, has become morally and realistically bankrupt.

Safety and fear have only a partial relationship to external events, conditions and precautions. It is no wonder that the engineers and the lawyers cannot arrive at a satisfactory defini-

tion. Safety goes much deeper than machine guards, ZMS or
tort reform. Safety and the absence of fear are a product of
faith. Beyond all the reasonable precautions we can take, they
are ultimately bound together as attitudes of the heart and
mind that depend mostly upon the abundance of that inner
wealth which is offered in the Christian Gospel: "Perfect (or
mature) love casts out fear." (I John 4:18) This eventually
comes down to the maturity of our faith in something, or
someone beyond ourselves which fear itself can be a means of
discovering. As Lucy Bregman has put it, "God overcomes my
fears by turning them into pathways to him."

What does it mean to be safe and free from fear? It is the
sense of personal adequacy which the Apostle Paul had in
abundance, where he knew how to be abased and how to be
successful, how to live and how to die: "I can do all things
through Christ who strengthens me." (Philipp. 4:13) The Hebrew-Christian ethic confronts us with the chastening realization that we live in a world where calamity, accident and
stupidity are possible, and from which there is no absolute
external protection. We are reminded that we are responsible
for ourselves, as well as for each other. After we have done all
that we can externally, we must find our ultimate protection
from within. And it is here that this faith gives us the antidote
to fear and the need to be perfectly safe: not insurance, but
assurance that if we will indeed seek first the kingdom of God
and his righteousness all these things will be added in their
own good time and place.

Chapter 10

The Pathology of Greed

"Take heed, and beware of all greed (covetousness); for a man's life does not consist in the abundance of his possessions." (Luke 12:15) Jesus told a parable about a rich man whose land brought forth so plentifully he didn't have big enough barns to store it all. So he built bigger barns, and said to himself, "Soul, you have ample goods laid up for many years; take your ease, eat drink, be merry." But God said to him, "Fool! This night your soul is required of you; and the things you have prepared, whose will they be? So is he who lays up treasure for himself, and is not rich toward God." (Luke 12:16-21)

This is a perfect picture of the Greed Syndrome dominating the American marketplace and threatening the health of our nation. Sometimes this moral sickness is blatantly obvious. More often the line between a normal, healthy self-interest and a pathological greed is so subtle that this syndrome like a malignant tumor is present without our realizing it. Throughout our study the many symptoms of this ethical cancer have formed a series of patterns which tell a consistent story, and it is time now to pull them all together to determine its character and seriousness before going on to more positive therapy.

The Symptoms of the Greed Syndrome:

(1) The Rich Get Richer

Perhaps the most visible symptom of greed in our society is the awesome gulf between the rich and the poor. The extravagant life styles of "The Rich and the Famous," the unbelievable wealth of the *Forbes* 400, the inflated salaries, the instant lottery millionaires, the buccaneer windfalls on Wall Street, the multi-million dollar judgments in the courts, the 40 per cent contingency fees, the escalating insurance premiums, the high costs of medical service, all signal the kinds of abuses of wealth and status to which Jesus pointed: taking advantage of one's position to exploit others; selfish accumulation for personal satisfaction; showy substitutes for genuine ethical integrity; abusing the abundance of the earth for personal gain; wealth that in no way is a reward for righteousness. "Soul, you have ample goods laid up for many years. Take your ease; eat, drink, be merry." "Fool!" said Jesus. I am not impressed! Your life style stinks to heaven of ethical putrefaction! You are morally sick, and stand under the judgment of God! Strong words; but perfectly in keeping with Jesus' vigorous warnings to persons of wealth.

The greed phenomenon comes to particular focus when contrasted with the poverty and economic heartache becoming so poignantly visible in both rural and urban centers. As a recent denominational study put it: "The lustful power of affluence and the embrace of scarcity make a curious juxtaposition in our cultural values." When some gobble up more than they need, more than their fair share, then others must go hungry. We are learning that our economy, like our natural resources, is not an unlimited and bottomless reservoir. When some play the merger-mania game, then others must lose their jobs. When corporate raiders take over unwilling victims, then businesses are destroyed. When large industries leave the country to escape taxes and find cheap labor, whole communities are devastated. When clever arbitrageurs manipulate the stock market, then the small investors lose their life savings. When excessive litigation or the inability to find insurance destroys businesses, then a whole new dimension of poverty is created. When medical costs increase beyond the resources of socialized services then it is the poor who must suffer. The TV *Dallas* and Steinbeck's *Grapes of Wrath* are in increasingly violent contrast in America today. Symptoms of a widespread ethical sickness.

(2) The Cash Fixation: A Form of Prostitution

Money is a medium of exchange, a means to an end; but where the Greed Syndrome is operating it has become an end in itself. Cash money has become for many the primary measure of value. It is cash over useful products, cash over service, cash over quality, cash over the welfare of others. This is the escalation of the gambling mentality, where quick and easy cash is the measure of success, and the pushing of money around is turned into a desperate game. High yield means high risk, and the collapse of the stock market is just one illustration of where the risk factor has become pathological. Such materialism is almost always connected with short term thinking, with a fixation on the present and an ignoring of the future. The receiving of cash is equated with justice itself and the solution to all our problems. This cash mentality is anxiety-ridden, a form of slavery, a virus that infects the courts, the insurance system, and all of the professions. It is the prostitution of the American dream, representing a distortion of values and a falsification of reality that results in the bizarre symptoms we have been seeing. What we are describing is the worship of the god Mammon, complete with priests, temples and liturgies.

(3) The Overcrowded Professions

Another symptom of the Greed Syndrome comes in the

evidence that the professions producing the most money are
becoming overcrowded. Investment banking is the one that has
called the most attention to itself in recent days; but those of
law, medicine, entertainment, sports, science, and the upper
echelons of business have also been attracting some of our best
young people in this generation. The vocational focus has been
pulled away from those professions which contribute to social
value like education, or politics, or religion, or the fight against
poverty, immorality and crime. Is there really any question as
to why we are experiencing the worst escalation of crime in our
history? We get what we are willing to pay for in money, lives,
concern and dedication.

(4) Unredeemed Self-Interest

We have found self-interest and a concern for profit to be
a normal, useful and essentially healthy part of the human
endowment and in keeping with the Hebrew-Christian ethic.
But the problem is that without something to discipline and
re-orient this basic human drive, it quickly gets out of control
and becomes pathological. We have seen it operating in every
area where profit, efficiency and self are placed over other
persons and communities, over justice and morality, over principle and the traditional goals of a particular industry or
profession. The syndrome is identifiable as a climate where
individuals or whole professions take unfair advantage of others, demanding more than they need or deserve of this nation's
wealth. It is often characterized by a bizarre quality of perverse
unreality with expectations from others and from the system
that are as unbelievable as they are unfulfillable: "I must be
perfectly safe; I must not suffer; someone else must pay for my
trouble; I have a right to expect that manufacturers, doctors,
the government, indeed all with whom I deal, be perfect...ex-
cept, of course, myself." The monumental arrogance operating
here and evident in so many frivolous suits would be ludicrous
if it weren't so sinister.

(5) Fraud and Dishonesty

One of the more foreboding symptoms of this moral illness comes out in the fact that wherever we have found the Greed Syndrome in operation, without exception we have found an excessive amount of dishonesty, fraud and the deliberate breaking of the law. The one is the inevitable symptom of the other, like the pus that always accompanies infection. So much is this true that one test of the presence of the Greed Syndrome is whether or not a particular activity promotes or discourages dishonesty and integrity. There are situations, opportunities and attitudes within every profession, whether industry, Wall Street, law, insurance, medicine, the ministry or whatever, which, when combined with the prevailing antinomianism, have promoted a visible and sometimes extravagant outbreak of greed. The pervasive gambling mentality, operating as strongly on Wall Street as it does in the local lottery, is a particularly contagious atmosphere for the appearance of this symptom. Our state legislatures will one day wake up to the awful realization that they have invited a tiger into our homes.

(6) Hedonism

The pursuit of pleasure and the avoidance of pain is a natural and essentially healthy program. But it becomes pathological when it is paramount over a concern for God. It becomes diseased when it is superior to whatever values one has that transcend his or her own interests. It becomes destructive when it takes precedence over a concern for others, and an attention to the quality of one's product whether this be a manufactured good, a service, or the living of a life. "I must have it all. I must not suffer. I have a right to be reimbursed for my trouble. I am going to charge whatever the traffic will bear. I want something for nothing. Greed is good. Get what you can when and how you can." Don Juan, the prodigious lover, is in the saddle today with his ethic of quantity over quality, pleasure over pain, luxury over hardship, profit over principle. Whether in sex or in consumer goods, whether in court judgments, or the lavish exploitation of our resources, such hedonism is a collection of symptoms pointing to a deep moral illness. We are becoming a nation of hucksters and flabby-bodied, overweight, drug-laden, sexually perverted moral pygmies determined to squeeze every ounce of pleasure out of this highly endowed piece of global real-estate. "The great Satan," indeed! The Ayatollah is not a bad theologian. Jesus turned to Peter one day: "Get behind me, Satan! For you are not on the side of God, but of men." (Mark 8:33) There should be no wonder that we are in danger of losing our moral leadership before the world, or that conservative nations want no part of our culture.

(7) It Is Ultimately a Matter of Injustice

Of all the points of focus around which these virulent symptoms cluster, it is here that they come to the most lethal concentration. By ethical definition within the Hebrew-Christian tradition, greed is that which violates the justice of God. This is a formula for death.

(a) It is, first of all, a violation of God's sovereignty. Whenever there are evidences of what sociologists are calling radical individualism, aggressive self-actualization, or rampant humanism, we have a climate that promotes the self over everything else, over God, or others, or values, or high goals, and we can expect to see symptoms of greed. Grabbing more than we need or deserve violates God's lordship, for in this ethical tradition he has commanded us to be good stewards of his vineyard. If we put profit before principle, and short-term considerations over those of the long run we reject the divine perspective in favor of our own pitifully tiny set of concerns. Placing money over the things of the spirit comes, perhaps, to its most blasphemous form when justice itself is defined in terms of monetary awards. When money is equated with justice, then Mammon has dethroned the God of the Bible.

(b) The Greed Syndrome is also a violation of God's love. That violation has been seen in every area of this study. The placing of profit over persons is the basic symptom of the poverty of love. The lack of concern for the poor and the dispossessed accompanies the Greed Syndrome wherever it is found. The narrow conception of love that pits my own interests against all others, whether in the courts or in the market place, is widely symptomatic of that illness. The rejection of responsibility for others, and the attacking of the weak to my own advantage, are common expressions of the problem. The wreckage of broken relationships, the poisons of anger and hatred that emerge from unfriendly takeovers, the high costs of professional services and the acrimonious morass of litigation are the antithesis of God's love, and symptomize most poignantly our situation. The demand for reward irrespective of justice, the faithfulness of our service, or the quality of our product, is a radical misunderstanding of God's love and is another symptom of the Greed Syndrome. Equating love with sex and self-interest, we have debased the most precious possession of our Hebrew-Christian heritage. We have exchanged the basic ingredient of a healthy society, of marriage that works, and an economy that is truly productive, for a "mess of pottage" that is slowly poisoning us because it is filled with moral arsenic. *Eros* is its name and greed is its game. Social death is its end.

(c) Greed is also the rejection of God's wrath, one element of his justice that has largely been banished from the thinking of our generation. That rejection has created widespread confusion and done much to worsen the climate of greed. Parents have been afraid to punish their children. Schools have been fearful of imposing any real academic or social discipline upon their students. Courts have been reluctant to level stringent penalties upon those committing crimes, or have been prevented from doing so by our legislative misunderstanding of the needed balance between love and wrath within the application of justice. But God is not mocked. His justice operates whether we recognize it or not. The downward spiral we have been observing of greed, dishonesty, crime, violence and social disintegration is the automatic operation of his wrath which is built into the very fabric of the universe.

(d) Our investigation has revealed that the freedom which is a necessary part of God's justice has been lifted out of context and made into an end in itself. Are we not "the land of the free?" Does this not mean that we can "do our own thing" without interference from a dictatorial government, or a nosy bunch of moralists spoiling our enjoyment of this supermarket of freedom?

It depends upon our ideology. If there is nothing beyond our own self-directed set of values, then there is no denying the logic of unrestricted freedom. But if indeed there is a God whose moral blueprint has been revealed to us then our fixation upon freedom is just the pitiful rebellion of morally immature children whose demand for license is justice out of balance and is a formula for disaster. In our greed, we have abused our freedom, using its opportunities to gobble up the riches of the land. We have enslaved others through poverty, or restraint of trade, or secret deals, or the coercions of greenmail and unfriendly takeovers. We have enslaved ourselves through the subtle imprisonments of fear or of greed itself as the bitterness and hatred we create isolate us from each other. And all of these are symptoms of the injustice of the Greed Syndrome and the inexorable operation of the justice of God.

(e) The evidence we have presented suggests further that we have allowed the administration of the law to take over the function of justice, while separating what is legal from what may be just, moral and right. In some courts we have created a lopsided justice where the plaintiff is supposed to win in product liability cases. And so we have narrowed the all-encompassing character of God's love. The prevalent belief that we have a right to break or ignore any law with which we do not agree is a naive rejection of the universality and faithfulness of God's law. And all these, too, are evidences of the operation of the Greed Syndrome; greed is a valid self-interest rejecting some aspect of the justice of God.

Understanding the Greed Syndrome

Bell called it "the megalomania of self-infinitization." I would call it simply an illustration of personal and social immaturity. One mark of maturity is the acceptance of the realities of one's self and situation. There are limits to what one can and should expect from life. If this is true, then one can see how unreal is the demand that "I must have it all." Greed, in one sense, is the refusal to accept the normal and inevitable boundaries within which a healthy life must operate. It is a form of self and social rejection which is one of the most prevalent symptoms of psychological disorder. The rejection of others and the realities of the world around us is really a rejection of ourselves. Psychiatrist Eric Fromme observed that, in his experience, selfishness is a form of self-hate, which is self-rejection in the extreme. It leads to living in a world of fantasy that can become strange, pathological and ultimately lethal. Bizarre suits that defy logic or justice, unreal expectations from doctors, courts and industries, fantastic life styles, promethean campaigns for profit, heavenly visions of pleasure and luxury, all point to living in a fantasia resembling Disneyland more than the real world in which we must live our lives. The Disney phenomenon is a welcome relief from reality. But when the American dream becomes this much out of proportion, we are into social pathology and society is sick.

The demands that have surfaced in this study that we should not be at fault for our own actions, that we should not have to face trouble or suffering or risk unless someone else pays us for it, are an extension of a nursery room mentality where "the one who dies with the most toys wins." The absence of moral responsibility is a clear symptom of the immaturity of an individual or a culture that has not gone beyond the most childish stage of self-interest into a mature and responsible concern for others. The excessive fears that operate within this

syndrome, prompting us to an extravagant and ultimately impossible pursuit of perfect safety, remind one of the excessive
anxiety of children afraid to go out in the dark. Immaturity is its
name. Our need is to grow up personally, socially and, most of
all, morally.

Systemic Versus Individual Evil

One of the more philosophical questions that lie behind
this Greed Syndrome has to do with the extent to which the
evil and injustice we are describing are a product of systems or
of individuals, and how much justice one can and should expect. New York theologian Reinhold Niebuhr alerted the last
generation to the problem in his book *Moral Man and Immoral
Society*. He convinced the scholarly world that one cannot expect justice from social systems, but only what he called "less
injustice." What this did was to separate personal ethics from
social ethics. This separation has become normative for this
generation. The prevailing pragmatism that ignores personal
ethical standards in American foreign relations is one illustration. The Greed Syndrome within the economic order is
another.

There has been a subtle and widespread support for the
separation between personal ethics and our conduct throughout the social scene that may well be influenced by the revival
of the old Lutheran doctrine of "orders," where each system or
order of society has its own ethical norms. One acts in business
in one way and in his or her home in another. Whether one
sees this in the massive book on ethics by Dietrich Bonhoeffer,
or in the more widely-read book by Niebuhr, the bottom line is
the same. You can't expect anything but highly flawed justice
from any system or "order" of society. It may well be that this
popular set of ideas has opened the door to the sleaze factor in
both the personal and social dimensions of our nation.

It is clear that we have been going through a period in our
ethical history where theologians and ethicists have been con-

centrating on systemic evil, and rightly so. The social problems of racism and poverty, crime and sexism, greed and substance abuse are painfully evident and obviously social. But, curiously, we have been reluctant until very recently to address ourselves also to the personal dimensions of these problems which have been considered off-limits to ethical examination. Private lives are private matters, and no nation should be able to interfere with or even criticize one's personal domain. We might even be sued for libel. Most remedies proposed for crime, drugs, fraud, stock market crashes, S&L bankruptcies and a host of other problems have been systemic, through legislation, litigation, social programs or stricter law enforcement. These are obviously in order. But as a result, our assessment of the sources of these various social diseases has been primarily sociological. And it has been inevitable that men and women would be encouraged to attribute their problems primarily, if not exclusively, to the social systems in which they operate or the social climates in which they live. Personal fault then becomes obscured behind a smokescreen of social factors. We are able to blame our problems on everyone and everything...except ourselves. Objectifying evil has always been a way for individuals to avoid personal responsibility. We are trapped in the system so our crimes are not our fault: our greed is a product of the times, the administration, the state of the economy, the competition, the inadequate laws, the various pressures on our lives. Such is the mentality we have seen within this Greed Syndrome.

The discoveries of sociologists and the insights of social ethicists in this generation have been dramatic and enormously helpful. But their very successes have diverted us from the necessary attention to the personal dimension. Ethics is indeed systemic, and we must address the systems in which we operate and correct their faults as far as that is possible. But within the Hebrew-Christian ethic the crux of the matter is not society but the individual human heart. We are judged by God not only as governments, or corporations or social groups but ultimately as individuals. Our motivations are intrinsically personal, our choices are essentially personal, our responsibility is basically personal, our punishment is finally personal. And unless we address the human heart, we never get to the heart of the problem. The present generation is discovering this ethical fact reluctantly but inevitably. The Boesky phenomenon and a rash of more recent indictments for insider trading, fraud and mismanagement hinge upon the moral-ethical choices of particular men and women. Personal and social ethics are inextricably bound together.

In recent years, the black community has been discovering the truth of that fact within the field of civil rights. We changed the system with all kinds of laws outlawing segregation and every form of discrimination and, in my opinion, this has helped enormously. But we have not yet conquered racism because this evil is not only systemic, but also intensely personal. The system was unjust. We changed that, and it has helped. But the hearts of too many men and women are still evil, filled with jealousy, hatred, greed, fear, prejudice and all the many personal problems that prolong the injustice.

The Bible, and especially the New Testament, makes a subtle but important distinction between evil and injustice. On this distinction hinges a vital ethical point. Jesus never used the word evil (*poneros*) for systems, but only for men and women. Systems, along with persons can be unjust, can reject God's love, ignore his wrath, avoid his commands and violate his freedoms in their programs, structures and actions. Jesus was intensely critical of injustice in his day. But only persons can be evil, for that is a description of the peculiar human capacity to reject the kingdom, the sovereignty, the presence of God from their innermost selves. Without that personal commitment, the justice of God loses its essential dynamic and is open to manipulation and distortion. In theological terms, evil is essentially existential. This is the "unforgivable sin" (Mark 3:29), the ultimate evil which rejects the "being," the Spirit, the presence of God.

Both the being and the nature of God are essential to the effectiveness of the Hebrew-Christian ethic. The prophet

Micah and Jesus each stressed this fact. The ethic of God's Word is a combination of both the doing of righteousness and the walking humbly with God, both the reflecting of God's nature and the experience of his sovereign presence. (Micah 6:8; Matt. 6:33) So it is that when systemic injustice is combined with personal evil, we have a moral-ethical crisis of epidemic proportions. The spark has hit the dynamite; another way of describing the Greed Syndrome. The problem is that it is just this personal dimension of religion and ethics, what I call the psychology of the kingdom (*RPG*-85), that has been neglected, rejected, downplayed and even ridiculed as outmoded piety in the last generation. Now we are paying for our sins. Theologian Edward Farley wrote the obituary in his book *Requiem For a Lost Piety*. Twenty years later these chickens are coming home to roost in a rash of individual indictments for fraud.

Pluralism and Moral Confusion

We have pointed many times in this study to the moral-ethical vacuum operating in our nation. Business men, lawyers, legislators, doctors, educators, even ministers don't say much about how we should or should not live in this generation. We have been so concerned not to offend each other that we have condemned ourselves to a terrible immaturity in our ability to sort out ethical matters. So often those convicted of dishonesty or fraud don't have a clue as to why their actions have been liable to prosecution, or even the subject of ethical criticism. The picture of Tammy Bakker is symptomatic, wailing to the nation over TV, "But I don't know what we have done wrong." Amorality is its name: woeful moral ignorance, the lack of an informed ethical conscience. By default, the ethical vacuum has invited a firestorm of self-interest and greed. The absence of moral instruction from our schools, the dearth of required courses in ethics within the graduate institutions of law, medicine, business and even our theological seminaries, is a travesty and an indictment of an ethically weak generation.

The situation has been vastly complicated by a phenomenon which is part of the very nature of American democracy and which has been growing rapidly in recent years. It is called pluralism, and has many sources in the religious and intellectual history of our nation. Most recently, with the increasing influx of foreign life styles, coupled with the fading of the dominant Hebrew-Christian ethic, we have entered a period where we are no longer a nation with clearly defined and generally accepted answers to basic questions on any subject. Orthodoxy, whether political, social or religious, despite the frantic efforts of the far right, is probably a thing of the past. This need not be a disaster. It could represent the very challenge that is needed to force us to new levels of social maturity. Whether we like it or not, pluralism has come to stay. How to handle it has become one of our chief problems, and we are ill prepared.

One way to identify this pluralism is in terms of what many have called radical individualism. This is a situation where more and more people are doing their own thing without much regard to what this does to others. The ethical result is what Bellah, in *Habits of the Heart*, has called "a solipsist value system." Moral relativism is another way of describing it. People act on the basis of ethical norms which they have made up, and for which they alone are responsible. Morals are therefore relative to one's own point of view. If Ivan Boesky thinks "greed is good," then who are we to say differently? Ethical pluralism is one of the chief sources of the confusion promoting the Greed Syndrome, and is one of the major challenges to American health and strength at this period in our history.

Functional Atheism

And the radical pluralists are right. That is, if it is true there is no God. Behind this ethical confusion lies the deepest concern of all. God has become a problem in America, and the

Greed Syndrome is essentially a form of atheism. What Robert Bellah calls "radical individualism," Daniel Bell "modernism" and Robert Benne "marketing hedonism," are all ways of referring to what theologian Gordon Kaufman refers to in his book *God the Problem*. As German theologian Paul Tillich put it a generation ago, we are a nation that has gone from a "theonomous" (God-centered) to a "heteronomous" (other-centered) culture. We are nominally believers in God as any Gallup poll will reveal. But in terms of what really motivates and guides our lives, we are mostly functional atheists.

The Apostle Paul identified the problem long ago: "although they knew God, they did not honor him as God." (Ro. 1:21) It was also Job's problem. He believed there was a God, but in his affluence he was really rebelling against him, having shifted his allegiance to the god of money. Like Job's experience, our modern atheism is so genteel, so good-natured, so surrounded by the trappings of religion, so well-disguised behind intellectual protestations and superficial morality that one has to look carefully to see the devil's ear protruding from our bourgeois respectability. But along every avenue of investigation in this study we have come to the point where the Greed Syndrome has been seen as a form of atheism. Our capitalism has lost the God who formed the heart of John Calvin's vision, and so provided the center and basic stability for this new form of economics.

Functional atheism is seen in two fundamental ways. It is first of all reflected in the radical individualism that puts self-interest ahead of others and God. It refuses to accept our wealth as a trust over which we are commanded to be good stewards, and so worships money, profit, quantity, pleasure, luxury, safety, litigation and the laws of economics in the place of God. We have rejected the lordship of God over our lives, and so denied his essential sovereignty. Symptomatic is the current use of the divine name. A generation ago some theologians, influenced by the linguistic schools of philosophy, were having trouble even pronouncing the divine name. They urged that we only spell it out, "G.O.D." Today, according to a recent commercial, G.O.D. means "Guaranteed Overnight Delivery" and is the name of a trucking company making a lot of money.

Secondly, our atheism is seen in Job's rejection of God's justice. We have created our own version of God who is a benevolent Deity whose infinite indulgence is a mirror of our own self-interest. We have created God in our own image. The Greed Syndrome is a description of our lopsided, self-serving, inadequate view of God's nature. Again, in this study we have in every area of investigation concluded that the Greed Syndrome is ultimately a description of a valid self-interest out of tune in one way or another with the justice of God . The major problem with the God of this generation is that he is a God of unconditional love, whose infinite indulgence has deadened his wrath with its demand for responsibility, whose benevolent "Yes" has drowned out his warning "No," and whose facile goodness has left us unable to cope with the existence of evil and suffering in the world. He is a God of unlimited liberation whose extravagant cornucopia of freedom has all but swamped the sober, restraining imperatives of his law. He is not a God of justice as we find him described on almost every page of the Bible, but a God created in our own image and refashioned into the likeness of another god called Mammon.

In the light of the Hebrew-Christian ethic, not honoring God as he has been revealed to us is the most subtle and prevalent form of atheism. This is the heart of the Greed Syndrome, and our most basic problem. The agony of our illness is the problem of how to handle our vulnerability in a no-God world. If we cannot know or accept God on his own terms, then we do not know how to act in any way that can hope to transcend our own narrow self-interest and be in ethical tune with the universe as it really is. If there is no clear knowledge of the nature of God, then there are no ethical absolutes. Each man and woman must be the arbiter of what is right and wrong, what is just and unjust.

Children of Hell: the Devil and His Angels

In Biblical terms, we have been descending into hell. Biblical hell is not some awful grotto in the center of the earth. It is the deep night of the soul, that condition of personal existence where God is absent. (*RPG*, 95-115) Jesus referred to those living in the darkness of God's absence as "children of hell." (Matt. 23:15) And he so identified on the cross with men and women rebelling against God that he impaled himself on that most basic problem of the human condition: "My God, my God, why have you forsaken me?" (Mark 15:34) Jesus answered his own question some days before as he paused to survey the city of Jerusalem spread out before him: "O Jerusalem! How often would I have gathered your children together as a mother hen gathers her chicks, but you would not. Behold, your house is forsaken!" (Matt. 23:38) God's wrath is his rejected love. He has not forsaken us, but in his justice allowed us to forsake him if we must. The Apostle Paul called this God's giving us up to ourselves. (Romans 1:24f.) There is no more just or awful judgment. The Greed Syndrome is the ethic of hell, a system of values based, however unconsciously, upon the rejection of the sovereignty and justice of God. The distilled essence of this ethical virus is the bitter cup of what the Bible calls "the wrath of God, prepared for the devil and his angels." It is a deadly poison.

In modern economics, it translates into the very symptoms of the Greed Syndrome we have been examining: self-actualization as an end in itself, profit over principle, money before the things of the spirit, self over others and God, no fault or responsibility, demanding more than we need or deserve, exaggerated expectations, expediency, opportunism, dishonesty, taking unfair advantage of the weak. These are in and of themselves the punishment of God's wrath, the very shadow of hell casting its somber darkness over our lives.

Economic Nihilism

The Russian novelist Fyodor Dostoevsky in his essay, "Notes From Underground," describes a man who spends his life underground in the darkness which is symbolic of his despair. That is all he has and, eventually, he comes to love the dark. Albert Camus, in *The Stranger*, describes a man whose life has lost its hope before "the benign indifference of the universe," and whose final happiness is the realization that at his execution there would be a huge crowd of spectators who would greet his twisting body with howls of execration. In another book, *The Myth of Sisyphus*, Camus describes the mythical character who is condemned to push a large rock up a hill for all eternity. Just when he reaches the top, it rolls back to the bottom where he must begin the process all over again. For Camus, this is all there is to life. And as he looks into the abyss of nothingness at the heart of the universe, he finds some comfort in a scream of protest against the absurdity of it all.

Finding meaning in despair while twisting in the wind or pushing a rock up a hill are all expressions of the philosophy of the absurd which arose in Europe after World War II. It was an existential philosophy of despair based upon the absence of God. These philosophers looked deeply into life, and that means into their own hearts, and found only an abyss of nothingness, the realization that in a no-God world there is no hope, no salvation. We must make it on our own. And this is absurd. Jean Paul Sartre in his novels counseled suicide as the only way out. Camus rejected this and with a relentless honesty and courage proposed an unrelenting scream of protest.

Many disillusioned people in post-war Europe and America have identified with this mood. In art, literature and drama they have tried to express this philosophy of nihilism, where nothing really matters. Without God or hope or meaning, it is all absurd, merely twisting in the wind. Protest has meaning for its sake alone. Extravagant self-indulgence or the deadening of consciousness through alcohol and drugs are all forms of self-destruction. In themselves they provide a certain meaning in the endless night of God's wrath. Absurd theater, art and literature are attempts to express this existential vision of the meaninglessness of life. What they portray is cultural suicide.

The Greed Syndrome has many of the characteristics of the absurd. It is spawned in the deep night of God's absence. Its offspring are children of unlimited self-interest who find meaning through the aggressive pursuit of wealth, pleasure and the prostitution of the gifts of the earth. Its style of frivolous suits, unrealistic expectations, extravagant wealth, economic warfare, quantity without quality, constitute an economic theatre of the absurd. It finds meaning in the pushing around of money, without value or product; it has no logic except that of the absurd because it is out of tune with the center of logic which is the justice of God. The rapacious epidemic of mergers and unfriendly takeovers, of arrogant litigation and the frantic pursuit of wealth is Camus's scream of defiance at the dark night of economic nothingness. The dishonesty, fraud, self-interest and lack of concern for moral values typical of this syndrome is Sartre's formula for self-destruction. Economic Nihilism is its name.

A Sickness Unto Death

Ivan Boesky once explained to an interviewer why he kept on frenetically risking millions long after he had made more than he could spend in several lifetimes: "It's a sickness I have in the face of which I'm helpless." (*Barrons*, Nov. 24, '86, 6l) This bit of prophetic "sinsight" is an apt description of the present state of our economy. It is ethically sick. Basil Mitchell put the problem profoundly in his Gifford lectures at Oxford, published under the title *Morality, Religious and Secular; the Dilemma of the Traditional Conscience.* (Oxford, '80) "A moral tradition becomes ossified or disintegrates as it increasingly becomes divorced from the world view which provides its ultimate rationale."

The capitalist system combines two creative but dangerous

ingredients: a) a system based on human self-interest, with the most efficient source of profit ever devised; b) a system based upon an obsessive commitment to human freedom that is the envy and the fear of the world. Under control, these are healthy and creative forces; but they are prone to abuse and are susceptible to personal and social disease. Greed is a diseased profit motive. Corruption is a diseased freedom. The moral antibodies within capitalism that control this chronic malady are the elements that comprised the Protestant Ethic: honesty, integrity, hard work, responsibility, restraint and law; most of all, a strong commitment to the sovereignty and justice of God. There will always be greed and corruption in the world, just as there will always be germs to threaten the health of the body. But as long as the moral white corpuscles are strong enough to fight the disease, to neutralize and restrain it, the corporate body remains healthy.

We are suffering today from an epidemic of moral AIDS. Our ethical immune system is breaking down. The name of this disease, as it appears in the economic sector, I have called the Greed Syndrome. There are many who are pointing to the possibility of economic and social disaster. And the symptoms are severe enough to justify the warning. In this generation, fraud and corruption in America have staggered the international economy. Dishonesty and excessive risk have contributed to the steepest plunge in stock market history. The merger-mania with its epidemic of unfriendly takeovers, leverage buyouts, junk bond financing and deep pocket litigation has put our industry in such trouble that we have lost our world leadership in one area after another. We have become the most "sue-happy" nation on earth; our medical profession is being seriously crippled, and the insurance industry is in the worst crisis in its history.

We have been forced to learn, in these post-war days of our world dominance, that America is neither infinitely prosperous, militarily invincible nor politically invulnerable. And the time for self-realization has come. We have become morally and socially weak from a disease that is prone to attack a capitalist economy. We are the target for every nation, power group and special interest on earth. It is a moral morass, a cancer spreading throughout the body. The Mafia and the international drug lords, the insider traders and corporate raiders, greedy men and women in every profession, like predatory animals, are attacking us at these very points of our greatest weakness. It is my impression that they still represent a minority of Americans. But the disease is spreading rapidly, and it is time for all of us to clean up our part of this ethical Three Mile Island. It is a moral pollution problem of catastrophic dimensions, a sickness which, if not treated effectively, could lead to economic, social and moral death. There is still probably no nation on earth able to destroy America. The only one that could do that is America herself. The most dangerous question coming from our study is this: is America committing moral suicide? We are probably too strong to die, but we could become a moral and social invalid as many of the great civilizations of history have done in the past, malingering into mediocrity.

The Moral Iceberg

The Greed Syndrome is but the tip of the iceberg in the mountain of ethical problems threatening this nation "under God," which has gotten out from under God's sovereignty in recent generations. It is a set of symptoms identifying one aspect of the much larger sleaze wave of degeneration in the faith and morality of America. All the symptoms come together at this point: putting money and self ahead of God and others. Greed is the appearance in the economic life of the rebellion against God which is the primary fuel and occasion for every kind of sin. Behind most, if not all, perversions of sex, money, drugs, violence, war, and our general inhumanity to each other, lies the fact that we are human beings free to rebel against God, and prone to do so in every way we can. So what we have said about greed is related to a host of other problems as America faces an ethical epidemic more serious than drugs, aids or cancer.

The Presbyterian General Assembly recently expressed the urgency of this moral crisis as a time of general ethical disarray. It involves a new notion of humanity deeply antithetical to our Christian convictions; a culture gone radically skewed in its values, "fraught with danger and irrational expectations." We stand under the judgment of God. The only answer to an essentially moral question is a moral answer. Ultimately, greed does not work. It is a disaster waiting to happen because it is out of tune with the justice of God. So Jesus' response to a question posed earlier is still this: No, you cannot serve both God and Mammon. The only way to bridge the awesome black hole between God and greed is to take Mammon into God's service. Therein lies our hope.

Chapter 11

The Tactics of Hope

Now let's turn the whole analysis over, for we have been looking primarily at the underside. If this recital of greed and personal-social immaturity were all there were, then there would be no hope. Perhaps we should then join the rush to gorge ourselves with the fruit of the land before the whole wretched mess goes up in flames. In the words of an enigmatic sign on the wall of a Florida real estate development, "Enjoy yourself; it is later than you think."

But this is not a litany of despair. There is more. The despairing nihilists are wrong. The philosophers of the absurd are wrong. The merchants of greed are wrong. There is hope, and it is based not on some clever human scheme, but upon the most important singular fact of the universe. There is a God of justice in whom we can find our hope. This is the ultimate message of the Bible. Hope comes not only from understanding the pathology of greed, but most especially from understanding, accepting and applying the therapy of the only Power which has the sovereign ability to chastise, heal and redeem.

> "Why are you cast down, O my soul,
> and why are you disquieted within me?
> Hope in God; for I shall yet praise him
> my help and my rock." (Psalm 42:5)

Reveille For a Biblical Life Style

We live in a time of the shortage of power. The tragic blindness of our age is that we do not understand the kind of power we need. The power we are looking for is the power to raise the value of the dollar. The power we really need is the power to raise the level of our values. The power we are looking for is the power to clean up the land and sea and air; but the most serious pollution problem is that of mind and heart. The power we are looking for is the power to alleviate poverty; but the power we most desperately need is the power to alleviate our poverty of spirit. It is to this kind of power that the Bible most exactly speaks.

I have expressed some of the details of such Biblical therapy at many points in the context of a particular problem. Now it is time to gather these insights together into a therapeutic whole. They tell a consistent story of ethical ideology, strategy and tactics, revolving around the sovereignty and justice of the Biblical God. In this chapter, we are most concerned with tactics, with the method for the practical application of the Hebrew-Christian ethic to the economic scene. I offer the following as a program for making ethical decisions that are in tune with the nature of the moral universe as it is described in the Bible. At every point, the Hebrew-Christian ethic is the reverse of the Greed Syndrome.

We Must First Distinguish Between the Jewish and the Christian Ethic

When we get to the tactical level of any ethical problem, it is necessary to focus more exactly on a particular approach and to be consistent in it if the method is to be effective. It is at this point that differences between the Hebrew and the Christian ethical traditions are especially evident.

The method that came out of the Hebrew synagogue during the Babylonian exile was that of code morality. The central law-giver was Moses, and the chief figures were the rabbis who acted as interpreters of the law. The method involved a strict adherence to the written word. Ethical decisions were made in terms of rabbinic opinions on specific cases. This is called "case law," or casuistry, and is essentially the model followed by our American civil courts. In such an approach, the decisions of the most respected judges, or significant cases, become the guide for future interpretations of the law. Over the years this has evolved into a large body of legal opinions which have been gathered into collections like the Mishnah for the Jews, and large law libraries for the American court system. The Jew has called this "Torah." For the observant, it has become a guide for every aspect of life.

What happened with the Jews in the first century, but not necessarily in later times, was that the debate over tactics tended to replace a concern for strategies or ideology. For example, how many ashes could one take out of his fire without dishonoring the Sabbath day? The administration of the written codes or precedents, what the Jews of Jesus' day called "the traditions of the Elders," took over the function of justice and questions like this were debated endlessly. This is what has happened to American civil law, and is, I think, one of its chief problems. The administration and interpretation of the written codes and precedents have replaced a more total concern for justice. The assumption is that they are the same. But we have found in this study many cases where that does not seem to be true. Jesus put it to the synagogue lawyers of his day: "You tithe mint, rue and cummin; but you neglect the weightier things of the law. Justice and righteousness: these you ought to have done without neglecting the others." (Luke 11:42)

The Christian ethical tradition, on the other hand, follows the Hebrew prophets rather than this early synagogue approach and accepts the teachings of Jesus, what the early Christians called "the holy word," as the basis of the Church's thought and practice. Jesus allied himself with the prophetic tradition which was less legalistic than that coming from Moses and more based upon the spirit of God than upon the written

code. The Jewish Torah is not rejected but accepted with res-
ervations, and then complemented in some significant ways.

Jesus accepted the justice of God presented by the prophets as a basis for an ethic that is always true in every situation.
What he did with ethics, as with everything else he borrowed
from the Old Testament, was to spiritualize it, universalize it
and add himself as the fulfillment of Torah. (*JGTJ*, 237f.) Jesus
insisted that, "I came not to destroy the law, but to fulfill it."
(Matt. 5:17) So he often quoted Moses but then regularly
added his own fulfilling insights: "You have heard that it was
said, 'You shall love your neighbor and hate your enemy.' But
I say unto you, Love your enemies and pray for those who
persecute you, so that you may be sons of your Father who is in
heaven...." (Matt. 5:43-45) The emphasis on love is one of
Jesus' chief contributions to the Hebrew understanding of
God's justice.

The Apostle Paul spent his life examining the differences
between Judaism and Christianity. In his letter to the Gala-
tians, he came to a particularly clear expression of what has
been standard for Christianity ever since: "For freedom Christ
has set us free; do not therefore fall back into a yoke of slavery
...Walk by the spirit; if you are led by the spirit, you are not
under the law." (Gal. 5) What Paul was warning against was the
problem that comes when religion and ethics are seen as a
slavish devotion to a mass of written rules and precedents. The
Jews had amassed over 1500 rules for the observance of the
Sabbath day alone. "Freedom in the Spirit" was Paul's ethical
explanation of what Jesus was saying in his teaching about
basing one's life on God's sovereign love rather than on a rigid
list of do's and don'ts. So the Christian ethic is not a legalistic
ethic. It has a built-in uneasiness with regard to any ethical
system based on a code and administered through case law.

The Distinctively Christian Ethical Tactics

What the Christian ethic does propose is an ethic based on

three principles. It is first of all an ethic founded upon a set of relationships to God, to self, and to others whose controlling power is the Spirit of God and whose guiding principle is love. (Mark 12:28-34) The Apostle Paul called it being "in Christ," and "walking in love." (Eph. 5:2) Such freedom in the Spirit places us under a new kind of loving constraint: "You who were once slaves of sin have become obedient from the heart ...slaves of God." (Ro. 6:17) The Christian ethic is the expression of a divine-human love affair. It begins at a very personal level, with men and women on their knees before God. In this sense, an ethical life is essentially the overflow of a vital experience of the loving presence of God.

Secondly, this ethic is committed to the absolute validity, adequacy and necessity of the justice of God. This comes from the revelation of God's word within the Hebrew-Christian experience. As we have seen throughout this book, revelation can be crystallized into a series of ethical strategies which act as general principles rather than specific rules. Its function as an absolute standard for ethics depends upon the acceptance of that word as valid, adequate and absolutely necessary.

Thirdly, the Christian ethic is a process of growth to maturity in love. Religious commitment does not automatically produce moral giants. We are reborn into God's kingdom as babes in need of moral and spiritual growth. Jesus talked in terms of bearing the "fruits" of the kingdom of God, and these come only from mature plants. (Matt. 5-7) Paul liked the word *teleios* to describe the Christian ethical goal. It means perfection, or more accurately, maturity: "For this I strive...to present every man (and woman) mature (*teleios*) in Christ." (Col.1:28) For Paul and Jesus, ethical acts are more or less mature, in terms of God's lordship over our lives, our understanding of divine justice, and our skill in applying it.

So in dealing with ethical questions in a Christian context, I am uneasy about answering the question, "What is right or wrong?" in some absolutistic sense. Rather, I prefer to re-phrase this into the more Christian question which gathers up the essence of the other: "What is more or less mature in love?"

Maturity in love is the method for making ethical decisions which I have already introduced to help us grow up economically and in every other way into the kinds of persons who can handle the ethical demands of a highly pluralistic society. It has informed every page of this book. Now we can expand it and use it as a means of pulling together the practical, therapeutic insights that have emerged throughout our study.

Maturity in love is a way of acting ethically that combines ethical ideology and strategy into a working whole. It combines that which is always true with what depends on the situation; that which is certain with what must be tentative; that which is rational with what is highly relational and even emotional. Its particular genius is that it enables us to operate in a highly varied culture with sensitivity to all while at the same time being true to our own convictions.

The heart of this method lies in Jesus' directions to his disciples to love God, self, and others, "with all your heart, and with all your soul, and with all your mind, and with all your strength." (Mark 12:28-34) Here is a total program involving all that we are, emotionally, intellectually and physically, and directed to all three of the sets of relationships in which we operate, whether we admit them or not. The key is to reflect the person and nature of God totally in our lives, what Paul called "glorifying God." (I Cor. 6:20) The central concept of love operates within the larger framework of the justice of God as we have described it. When applied to ethical tactics, it becomes a program aimed at the expression of these three relationships through three avenues of communication that involve all that we are as human beings in our reason, our emotions and our physical actions. These avenues are *understanding*, *acceptance* and *expression*, and are similar to the standard practice of modern psychiatry, which, through men like Freud and Jung, is heavily indebted to the Bible. To chart the method might look like this:

Maturity in Love

To Whom?	With What?	How?
God	Mind (Reason)	Understand
Self	Heart and Soul (Emotion)	Accept
Others	Strength (Body)	Express

The Upward Look

The Christian ethic begins by taking an upward look to God. Even as we look down in prayer, so we are looking up to God. Already we have done something that is usually ignored in making ethical decisions. This is partly because of the current functional atheism that denies the existence of ethical values that go beyond those of any particular person, group or generation. It is also a product of our lack of understanding of what God might have to say to a particular problem. His justice is so massive, and our problems so detailed that it is hard to bring them together. So we need to break down our understanding of God's sovereignty and justice into its component parts and apply them specifically to our human problems in order to be able to "Do justice" and "Walk humbly with our God."

To begin this upward look, the Hebrew-Christian ethic revolves around two poles: the being of God as sovereign lord and the nature of God as justice. In the statement which has become central to this whole study, Jesus put it simply, and applied it to economics: "Seek first the kingdom of God and his righteousness (or justice), and all these things will be yours as well." (Matt. 6:33) What this ideological summary tells us is that ethical living which is in tune with the created universe is the reflection in one's life of the being (kingdom) and nature (justice) of the Creator himself. It is the only moral absolute in the Christian ethic.

Christian ethical tactics are called faith, and involve all

three of these avenues of relationship. *Understanding* God is a matter of belief, and is primarily rational. It is here that an intellectual grasp of the sovereignty and justice of God informs the search for ethical absolutes, for ethical norms that are always true whoever you are or wherever you live. *Accepting* God is an act of trust, and includes the more emotional activities of prayer and worship. *Expressing* God is a life of obedience, and involves demonstrating in our actions his justice and sovereignty. Such knowledge, acceptance and expression do not come easily. We are all students of his word, at varying levels of maturity, whether we know it or not, or by whatever name we call ourselves. For there are no absolute atheists, but only those who deny with their lives what they know to be true in their minds and hearts.

Understanding the Strategies of the Kingdom

All we have said about the strategies of God's sovereignty and justice come to play here at the beginning of this ethical process where ideology and strategy now become tactics. When it comes to applying a very large ideology to the specifics of any ethical question, we need a set of what the ethicist calls "middle axioms," implementing principles, what I have called strategies. These must be true to the particular ideology and be specific enough to be capable of application, yet flexible enough to be adaptable to the details of many different situations. The Old Testament provides some guidelines in the sermons of Moses which come to sharpest focus in the Ten Commandments. (Exodus 20) The New Testament ethic comes to particular focus in the teachings of Jesus in the Sermon on the Mount which contains an ancient summary in the Beatitudes. (Matt. 5:1-12)

There are also many other ethical insights running throughout the text of both Old and New Testament. These are not intended to be comprehensive or neatly organized. Scattered as they are throughout the Bible, it is very difficult for anyone but a serious student to apply them.

Seek First the Kingdom of God

The Kingdom of God is the concept Jesus used to pull together his thinking about every aspect of theology. Among many other things, this was Jesus' way of talking about God's sovereign presence in our lives. It was his way of describing what other New Testament writers preferred to call the Holy Spirit, and still others, like Paul, "Christ within you, the hope of glory." (Col. 1:27) This experience of the kingdom is the heart of prayer and worship and is primarily an emotional experience. Inevitably it has rational content which can be sharpened into ethical strategies.

1. The kingdom ethic means that the things of the spirit are more important than things of the material world. It is a matter of priorities, placing the entire economic enterprise secondary to the sovereignty of God.

2. The kingdom ethic says that principle is more important than profit. The bottom line is important, but must not be allowed to dictate policies. This is one of the most important contributions of the Christian ethic to economic success.

3. The kingdom ethic teaches us that there are things worse than death and more important than physical life. Human life is precious, but the justice of God in all of its facets takes precedence over the preserving, adorning and exploiting of human life.

4. The kingdom ethic recognizes that God's eternal plan is more important than temporal advantage. Translated into economics, it says that although expediency may have its place, long term considerations take priority over those of the short run. Inevitably, the Christian ethic is a future-oriented ethic.

5. The kingdom ethic insists that the quality of human life takes precedence over quantity. This can apply to standards in the work place as well as the life and character of persons.

6. The kingdom ethic looks below the surface to the inner

integrity of action and conviction. It is an ethic of the heart, where, as Jesus put it, "Out of the abundance of the heart the mouth speaks." (Matt. 12:34)

7. The kingdom ethic is a priority of relationships, putting God first, the other person second, and self last.

"Do Justice, Seek First...His Righteousness"

Justice is the chief Biblical description of what God is like. As such, it is primarily a rational concept and so lends itself particularly well to the formulation of ethical strategies. What God demands is that we reflect his nature in our ethical lives. As we have pointed out many times, God's justice includes four very large concepts. The Biblical ethic demands first of all their understanding, then their acceptance, and finally their expression as the guiding rule of our lives. All three activities tend to go on together and mutually enforce or hinder each other.

A. The Love of God As Ethical Strategy

Love is God's essential nature. As the author of I John put it, "God is love." (45:8) To know God is to love him. This, too, can be translated into economic terms.

1. Love that reflects the nature of God, which the Bible calls *agape*, is permissive, aggressively deferring to the beloved. It is characterized by faithfulness and a persistent regard that permits persons to express themselves in ways that are fulfilling. A loving situation is one where there is an abundance of goodwill that overflows with a supermarket of benefits.

2. Such love is concerned to provide appropriate rewards for righteousness. People must know that if they work nobly, sacrificially, and do their best, there will be fitting compensation for their faithfulness. This may be in financial terms, but the fruits of the Spirit are characteristically much more lasting

and satisfying. Paul described them as love, joy and peace. (Gal.5:22)

3. This love demands the concern to provide sources of help for individuals and institutions that make achievement of the good life possible.

4. Any situation based on the love of God requires some possibility for forgiveness. There must be opportunity for a second chance, for expunging the record, for restoration.

5. Love that reflects the justice of God is faithful, based upon a lasting covenant. Translated into economics, this means a continuation of our regard for others beyond expediency and the necessities of the immediate situation.

6. Love is a relationship that points us toward the development of loving relationships with all, beyond the confines of our own social, economic or national circle.

7. Love is a matter of the heart and must be induced rather than coerced. As a relationship, it seeks the establishment of such relationships between all persons within the economic structure.

B. The Wrath of God As Ethical Strategy

The wrath of God in the Bible is his punishment for sin, his willingness to allow for suffering in the world, his love in agony, allowing men and women to exclude him from their lives if they must. It is God's willingness within his justice to allow us to be greedy, but insisting that we bear the punishment of our choices. It has enormous practical meaning for economics.

1. The wrath of God demands punishment for sin. Without this, love becomes overly permissive and situations degenerate in the imbalance of their injustice.

2. The wrath of God demands restraint because men and women are by nature created to serve their own interests. This legitimate concern for self-preservation quickly becomes perverted by all that constitutes the erotic and demonic within human nature.

3. A just wrath must be redemptive. It must not be vengeance for itself alone, but aimed at therapy and redeeming the particular situation.

4. The wrath of God embraces the mystery of suffering, inequality, poverty, calamity and death. In Biblical terms these are not evil. They are the price of our humanity and freedom. They are all part of living as intelligent creatures in a universe governed by natural law. The only evil (*poneros*) in the teachings of Jesus is men and women rebelling against God.

5. But the wrath which admits these possibilities must be in tension with God's love which demands concern for the plight of the distressed and is dedicated to the redemption of the inevitabilities of our humanity. God's love always redeems his wrath.

C. The Command of God As Ethical Strategy

Wherever God is presented in the Bible, there is a "thou shalt" or a "thou shalt not." This is the expression of his sovereignty. He does not ask our permission or beg our pardon. He commands. We do not elect him. He does not abdicate, nor can we impeach the Almighty. The universe runs according to his will, and we ignore him at our peril. Translated into economics, this becomes the driving force of the Hebrew-Christian ethic.

1. God's justice is a coherent, orderly structure brought to clear focus in a law-abiding universe. Human society, in order to function effectively, must reflect the ordered rationality of God's law. When it does not, the symptoms of lawlessness and absurdity signal the breakdown of justice.

2. For God's justice to be expressed in human relations, law must be in proper balance with love and wrath, and with the freedom he gives us to obey or disobey.

3. God's imperative implies that the absolute command to do justice be a permanent one, not limited to any age or temporal condition. We cannot suspend it for a moment without

reaping the dire consequences of justice out of balance.

4. God's imperative is also universal, not limited to any race, sex or social condition. To direct it primarily to one group at the expense of another is not to right the balance of justice, but to further extend its imbalance with the inevitable creation of still more injustice.

5. For law to be just, it must be obeyed. The rule of law must be established in every area of life and, having been established, must be enforced if justice is not to be perverted. Law that is not enforced inevitably leads to the downward spiral of frustration, bitterness, dishonesty, violence and some form of death. We never break a law of God; we always break ourselves against it.

D. The Freedom of God As Ethical Strategy

Freedom is that aspect of God's justice that makes us able to be human. We have the intelligence to make essential decisions, and this separates us from the animals. Our most essential freedom is to reject the will of God. The awesome ethical implication is that we have not only the power to destroy ourselves, but also cur economy and the planet on which we live. That power can be sharpened into certain ethical strategies.

1. Since freedom is an expression of the nature of God, it is also one of the most basic needs of the human personality. To suspend it in the name of something less than the cause of justice is to condemn that situation to the disaster that always accompanies injustice.

2. There must be a freedom to sin if one wills; to make important choices that go against one's best interests if that is the decision. The over-solicitous concern to prevent any society or individual from making bad choices is a denial of basic freedom. This injustice will ultimately not work. Mistaken idealism is usually the beginning of tyranny.

3. Justice also demands the freedom to do good, if that is

one's decision. Whenever the freedom of some to break God's moral laws impinges on the freedom of others to obey them, this, too, is a denial of basic freedom. Such injustice will trigger penalties which are built into the very situation itself.

4. Freedom is not an ideal that stands alone. Nor can it be safely or effectively separated out from the total fabric of God's justice. In order to work, it must operate within the complete framework of law, punishment and love.

The Higher Pragmatism

For the justice of God to be present, all four of these great facts of the moral universe must be in operation. It is the dynamic tension of their togetherness that produces the kind of health, prosperity and salvation offered in the Bible. It is only when life is just that it works in the wonderful and effective ways God intended. Throughout this study, whenever we have identified a set of particularly pathological symptoms of the Greed Syndrome, there we have found some aspect of God's justice either missing or out of balance. In particular, in this age, the imbalance has been the fixation upon freedom and the rewards of love to the exclusion of law and the restraints of punishment. We want to squeeze the rich juices out of life and go swimming in them without any interference from requirements or penalties. But this is not possible.

So I would propose that we turn over the humanist pragmatism of John Dewey that builds a philosophy on the dictum, "whatever works is right," and supplant it with God's higher pragmatism as we find it in the Bible: *"whatever is right (just) will work."*

If there is indeed such a God who has revealed himself to us, then there is no possibility for a viable ethic aside from a strong relationship to him. This is why atheism is such a serious source of ethical weakness in America. So Jesus commands his disciples to take first of all the upward look to God. We must reflect God's sovereignty and justice in our lives simply because he is creator and we are creation. There is no other justification given in the Bible, nor is any needed. Without it, there can be no ethic that either transcends the evil of mankind or is in tune with the moral laws of creation.

The Inward Look

Looking within ourselves with honesty and candor is another necessary part of growing to psychological maturity, and so it is with ethical decisions. In our study we have seen how the aggressive human *eros* with its drive for self-fulfillment, profit and priority can dominate our lives and warp our ethical judgments. What the New Testament ethic insists is that this basic *eros*, which is all self-interest, must grow up. *Eros* must become *philia*, translated friendship, which is a more mature concern for the welfare of others. This in turn must grow into more and more mature degrees of *agape*, the selfless love reflecting the very nature of God. Christians find this most perfectly revealed in Jesus' sacrifice on the cross. This is what the Apostle Paul means when he calls on all his readers to walk "in love" (Eph. 5:2), to "grow up" into "the measure of the stature of the fullness of Christ." (Eph. 4:13)

Understanding ourselves is not only knowing what we think and how we feel about things, but more importantly it is knowing *why* we think and feel that way. What prejudices, hurts and biases are operating within us to prompt a particular decision? An honest look within ourselves can tell us why we are making any particular ethical judgment, what it is doing to us, whether it is ennobling or debasing us, whether we really need what we are so determined to get, or whether this is just another tired expression of immature self-interest. And then we must accept the fact that this is the way we are, whether we like it or not. The failure to do this is called self-rejection, and is one of the most serious causes of misunderstanding, bigotry, hatred and men and women's inhumanity to each other. A simple psychological truth is an enormously important ethical fact: we hate and reject others because we first hate and reject ourselves. Understanding and accepting ourselves as we really are, that is, coming to love ourselves, is one of the basic clues to the emotional maturity which is true self-fulfillment, and the expression of our best selves. It is also the well-spring of mature ethical decisions.

The Outward Look

The Christian ethic calls for a mature love for others. In doing so, it demands that we put others ahead of ourselves. Tactically, this means that any ethical decision must be made in terms of the outward situation and what it will do to others. The realism of God's justice demands that we understand others, not as we would like them to be, but as they really are. Thus, communication is absolutely essential to a mature relationship.

Love also demands that we accept others on their own terms, allowing them to be themselves, accepting the fact that they are the way they are. This is the essential act of accepting people as persons with love and respect, even as we may be forced to reject what they do and stand for.

Maturity in love demands that we look honestly and accurately not only at institutions and situations but also at people without allowing our own prejudices to distort the reality. This tactical provision is one of the most commonly violated on the economic scene where our expectations are so often determined by our own desires without any understanding or acceptance of the needs of others and the realities of the particular situation or institution. Maturity in love does not mean that we have to agree with what others do, or approve of what they are. But it does mean that to deal maturely with people, with their associations and their problems, we must respect their right to be themselves, even as we might try to help them be better than they are. It is only through such acceptance that we can help others to express the best that is in them and in their situation. It is in this kind of maturity in love that the Hebrew-Christian tradition finds its highest fulfillment, and the Greed Syndrome its most potent source of healing.

God Is Alive and Well

The ultimate message of the Hebrew-Christian Bible is that even though our generation is ethically sick, God is alive and well. He is still offering us the antidote to the poison of greed. The wisdom of the Mosaic tradition, the inspired visions of the prophets, what Jesus called "the Word which I have spoken" (John 12:48) and the Apostle Paul "the light of the knowledge of the glory of God in the face of Christ" (2 Cor. 4:6), all constitute a body of religious experience through which shines the justice of God and in which we can find the power of his sovereignty. And from this theological, ethical, spiritual treasure, we can understand enough of the mystery of God's moral blueprint, and find sufficient resources for growing up into mature love, to have hope for the healing of the Greed Syndrome, and therapy for the sickness unto death of which it is a part.

"May the God of hope fill you with all joy and peace in believing,
so that by the power of the Holy Spirit you may abound in hope." (Ro. 15:13)

A Model for Doing Ethics Within a Hebrew-Christian
Context: Maturity in Love

The upward look to God

- Understand: God as he is
  God's kingdom sovereignty
  God's justice
  Love
  Wrath
  Command
  Freedom
- Accept God on his own terms
- Express God in obedience to his will

The inward look to self

- Understand ourselves as we really are
- Accept ourselves as we really are
- Express our best selves

The outward look to others, to situations, to problems

- Understand them as they truly are
- Accept them on their own terms
- Express the best that is possible with people and situations within all the above.

Bibliography

Abbreviations

JGTJ Baird, J. Arthur. *The Justice of God in the Teachings of Jesus*. Philadelphia: Westminster, 1963.

ACHJ Baird, J. Arthur. *Audience Criticism and the Historical Jesus*. Philadelphia: Westminster, 1967.

RPG Baird, J. Arthur. *Rediscovering the Power of the Gospel: Jesus' Theology of the Kingdom*. Wooster, Ohio: The Iona Press, 1982.

Selected Bibliography

Abt, Vicki, and others. *The Business of Risk, Commercial Gambling in Mainstream America*. Lawrence, Kansas: University Press of Kansas, 1985.

Auletta, Ken. *Greed and Glory on Wall Street, The Fall of the House of Lehman*. New York: Random House, 1986.

Barnett, Richard J. *The Crisis of the Corporation*. Washington: Institute for Policy Studies, 1975.

Bell, Daniel. *The Cultural Contradictions of Capitalism*. New York: Basic Books, 1976.

Bellah, Robert. *Habits of the Heart*. Berkeley: University of California Press, 1985.

Benson, George C.S. *Business Ethics in America*. Lexington, Massachusetts: D.C. Heath & Co., 1982.

Boesky, Ivan. *Merger Mania, Arbitrage: Wall Street's Best Kept Money Making Secret*. New York: Holt, Reinhart, Winston, 1985.

Braybrooke, David. *Ethics in the World of Business*. New Jersey: Rowman & Allanheld, 1983.

Calian, Carnegie Samuel. *The Gospel According to Wall Street, The Wall Street Journal*. Atlanta: John Knox Press, 1975.

Goldman, Alan. *The Moral Foundations of Professional Ethics*. New Jersey: Rowman & Littlefield, 1980.

Harrington, Michael. *Decade of Decision*. New York: Simon & Schuster, 1980.

Heilbroner, Robert L. *Business Civilization in Decline*. New York: W.W. Norton, 1976.

Hayden, Tom. *The American Future, New Visions Beyond Old Frontiers*. Boston: South End, 1980.

Jones, Donald G. *Business, Religion and Ethics, Inquiry and Encounter*. Cambridge, Massachusetts: Oelgeschlager, Gunn & Hain, 1982.

Kerr, Clark. *Work in America, The Decade Ahead*. Edited by Jerome M. Rostow. New York: Van Nostrand Reinhold, 1979.

Kreider, Carl. *The Christian Entrepreneur*. Scottsdale, Pennsylvania: Herald Press, 1980.

Kristol, Irving. *Two Cheers For Capitalism*. New York: Basic Books, 1978.

Lekachman, Robert. *Greed Is Not Enough*. New York: Pantheon Books, 1982.

Madrick, Jeffrey G. *Taking America*. New York: Bantam Books, 1987.

Mitchell, Basil. *Morality, Religious and Secular: The Dilemma of the Traditional Conscience*. New York: Oxford University Press, 1980.

Morris, Norval, and Gordon Hawkins. *The Honest Politician's Guide to Crime Control*. Chicago: University of Chicago Press, 1970.

Naisbitt, John. *Megatrends*. New York: Warner Books, 1982.

Novak, Michael. *Toward a Theology of the Corporation*. Washington: American Enterprises Institute, 1981.

Owensby, Walter. *Economics for Prophets*. Grand Rapids: Eerdmans Publishing Co., 1988.

Peale, Norman Vincent, and Kenneth Blanshard. *The Power of Ethical Management*. New York: William Morrow & Co., 1988.

Peters, Thomas J., and Robert H. Waterman, Jr. *In Search of Excellence*. New York: Harper & Row Publishers, 1982.

Raines, John C., and Donna C. Day-Lower. *Modern Work and Human Meaning*. Philadelphia: Westminster Press, 1986.

Rasmussen, Larry L. *Economic Anxiety & Christian Faith*. Minneapolis: Augsburg Publishing House, 1981.

Reeck, Darrell. *Ethics for the Professions, a Christian Perspective*. Minneapolis: Augsburg Publishing House, 1982.

Rifkin, Jeremy. *The Emerging Order*. New York: Putnam, 1979.

Ropke, Wilhelm T. *A Humane Economy, the Social Framework of the Free Market*. Chicago: Henry Regnery & Co., 1960.

Toffler, Alvin. *The Third Wave*. New York: William Morrow & Co., 1980.

Werhane, Patricia. *Profit and Responsibility*. Edited by Kendall D'Andrade. New York: Edwin Mellon Press, 1985.

Williams, Oliver, and John W. Houck. *Full Value*. San Francisco: Harper & Row Publishers, 1978.

Wogaman, Philip. *Economics and Ethics*. Philadelphia: Fortress Press, 1986.